HOW TO WATCH

ICE HOCKEY

A HANDBOOK FOR THE FAN

BY BERNIE WOLFE & MITCH HENKIN

© Copyright National Press, Inc. 1985, 1986, 1992
7200 Wisconsin Avenue
Bethesda, Maryland 20814
(301) 657-1616

Library of Congress Cataloging-in-Publication

Wolfe, Bernie, 1951-
   How to watch ice hockey.

   "A Full Court Press book."   Includes index.
   1. Hockey.   I. Henkin, Mitch, 1951-   II. Title.
GV847.W74   1985   796.96'2   85-13584
ISBN 0-915765-09-8 (pbk.)

Dedication

This book is dedicated to Patsy, Jennifer and Amanda Wolfe and to Marjan Henkin for their many sacrifices, encouragement and understanding.

Acknowledgments

The authors wish to thank those who contributed their time, thoughts and support: Lou Corletto, Pat Young, Mike Gartner, Bryan Murray, Ivan Labre, Kerry Fraser, Brad Kent, Stan Fischler, Dolores Adams, Gary Meagher, Dr. Allen Henkin, Neal Bobys and the public relations staffs of the Detroit Red Wings, Washington Capitals and the Montreal Canadiens.

Photos by Debbie Bell and Mike Althaus of the Photogroup, except where indicated.

Table of Contents

About The Authors

Bernie Wolfe played goaltender for the Washington Capitals hockey team from 1975 to 1979 and as a rookie in the National Hockey League (NHL), was the team's most valuable player (MVP). A Montreal native, he began playing the sport on the city's outdoor rinks at the age of six, and participated in the Montreal minor hockey system until entering college.

For four years he started in goal at Sir George Williams University (later renamed Concordia University) in Montreal, and was recently inducted into the school's hall of fame. During his collegiate career, he was the university's rookie of the year, was named to the Quebec all-star team three times and was all-Canadian his senior year. In 1974, he was named MVP in the Canadian Intercollegiate Athletic Union (CIAU) national championship tournament, equivalent to the NCAA final-four playoff in American basketball.

Bernie received his Bachelor of Commerce degree in 1974. He is a certified financial planner and president of Bernard R. Wolfe and Associates, Inc., a financial consulting company in Rockville, Maryland, representing 450 clients including many past and current NHL players.

Mitch Henkin graduated from Northwestern University in 1972 and obtained a masters degree in science journalism-communication from Boston University in 1976. From 1977 until 1981, he wrote regularly for the *Washington Post*. During that time, he covered a variety of sports and published many articles on sports medicine and racquet-sport instruction.

Henkin's first book, *The Racquetball Primer*, was published by the National Press in 1984. He currently teaches both tennis and racquetball in Bethesda, Maryland, and co-owns and directs TenniStar junior camps in that area. He is a member of the United States Professional Tennis Association and the American Alliance for Health, Physical Education, Recreation and Dance.

Foreword
Robert F. Fachet

As public opinion polls repeatedly tell us, hockey rates well down the list among fan favorites in the United States, a distant also-ran against the supremacy of football, baseball, basketball, tennis and golf. The sport's television ratings are so low that some stations decline to reveal them, with snide hints that there is nothing to reveal.

At the same time, no sport possesses such a fanatical following as hockey. An executive at a Washington television station once told me that he was fearful of any schedule change involving a telecast of the Capitals, because the switchboard was sure to be flooded with calls from irate — to put it mildly — fans.

Persons attempting to sell hockey in marginal U.S. cities like Washington, Atlanta, Denver and Pittsburgh have been buoyed by a statement considered gospel in hockey circles: If you can lure someone to the rink, you can hook him for life. In Atlanta and Denver, either that first game was a wrestling match against the Vancouver Canucks or ice remained fit only for mixing purposes in the minds of potential ticket buyers. The teams departed, to become the subjects of trivia questions.

In many other U.S. cities, however, hockey has attracted throngs of passionate fans, most of whom have similar characteristics. They root for the home team, love fights and haven't a clue of what is happening on the ice. Nothing is more entertaining to a person possessing true hockey knowledge than overhearing a so-called expert explaining the intricacies of the sport to a first-time fan.

When the Capitals came to Washington in 1974, I authored a series of explanatory articles, illustrated for eye-catching purposes by Sparky Schulz' Peanuts gang. I learned the difficulties of such an endeavor a couple of nights after I thought I had explained the ramifications of pulling the goaltender for an extra forward during delayed penalties. The visiting team lifted its goalie under such circumstances at Capital Centre, Washington's Hartland Monahan picked off a pass in front of the empty net and shot it in. Sirens wailed, lights flashed and fans screamed happily — until, of course, they learned it was no goal.

Bernie Wolfe has seen both sides of fans' passions. He has been saluted with cries of "Ber-nie, Ber-nie" from the Washington faithful. He also has been struck on the head — fortunately covered by a helmet — by a bolt thrown from the stands in Pittsburgh. In *How to Watch Ice Hockey*, Bernie has provided the most complete primer available to fans and would-be fans. Perhaps his book will help those who watch hockey to enjoy it more, and thereby raise the numbers of hockey fans in the U.S.

It's the kind of book that would make a fine gift for a potential fan, avoiding the embarrassment of a first-hand explanation at the rink. Before giving it away, however, take a read.

Introduction

Of all professional team sports, none moves along at a faster clip than ice hockey. Slap shots can travel at velocities in excess of 120 miles per hour, almost too rapid for the eye to follow. Players skate and crash at breakneck, racehorse speeds and strategy unfolds more suddenly than a full-court fast break in the National Basketball Association (NBA).

This quality makes the game exciting but can also bewilder novice ice-hockey fans. They are presented with a far more difficult task than faces their counterparts in other major-league sports.

For example, most spectators can absorb the basic premise of one of America's favorite pastimes, baseball, in an initial outing. It doesn't take long to learn enough to follow and appreciate the head-to-head confrontations between pitchers and hitters. But compared with the frenzied, nonstop progression of a hockey game, baseball unfolds in slow motion. Between batters and innings, plenty of time elapses for spectators to discuss the previous action.

In Canada and the northern cities of the United States, the weather stays cold long enough to make ice skating and hockey accessible and inexpensive. Kids, almost literally, grow up on the ice. Outside of those areas, hockey is often not as popular or as well understood as professional football, baseball and basketball. Frequently, both collegiate basketball and football draw better, attract higher television ratings and generate more local media coverage than do NHL teams competing in the same temperate locales.

The miraculous victory of the U.S. Olympic hockey team over the Soviet Union at Lake Placid in 1980 was witnessed by a mass television audience and exposed millions of Americans for the first time to the game's potential to evoke passion and unmatched excitement. However, the disappointing finish of the U.S. squad in the 1984 Olympics may have cooled that initial burst of enthusiasm on the part of the American public.

In cities like Pittsburgh, Los Angeles and Washington, where the home-team Capitals have acquired award-winning stars and have risen to championship-potential heights, thousands of regular-season seats remain empty for most games. Season tickets for National Football League (NFL) teams in those cities, on the other hand, are so highly sought after that they have become centers of controversy in divorce negotiations and are willed from parent to child.

The Pittsburgh Penguins averaged only 6,839 fans during the 1983-84 season, well below the league average of 12,000. During the 1984-85 season, Penguin forward Mario Lemieux scored 43 goals and totaled 57 assists to become the third NHL player to reach the 100-point plateau in his first year. That achievement won him the 1985 Calder Trophy as the league's top rookie and prompted *The Sporting News* to name Lemieux rookie of the year.

Despite Lemieux's performance, attendance still sagged. Team owner Edward DeBartolo Sr. set July 15, 1985, as a deadline for selling 10,000 season tickets, for the team to remain in Pittsburgh. The Los Angeles Kings, who made the 1985 playoffs, improved their attendance average to about 10,500 during the 1984-85 season, but still fell well below filling their seating capacity of 16,005.

Only a last-ditch effort spearheaded by the local business community saved the Capitals (who had net losses of $27.7 million in their first 10 years) from demise in the summer of 1982. Even after the "Save the Caps" campaign resulted in reductions in rent and county taxes, the hockey team lost more than $1.2 million in fiscal year 1983, according to Edmund Stelzer, comptroller for the Capitals.

Since that time, however, attendance, as well as the team's performance have improved dramatically. The Caps averaged a team-record 14,007 fans per game during the 1984-85 regular season, compared with 12,376 during the 1982-83 period. The number of Washington-area corporations holding season tickets rose from 15-20 to 75-80 during that span. Only recently the Caps, as well as several other American NHL franchises, have begun to create the broad-based fan support required to keep clubs on sound, fiscal ground.

The health of the NHL is not in question. It is nonetheless upsetting that during 1985, none of the NHL playoff series, including the Stanley Cup finals between Philadelphia and Edmonton, were broadcast nationally on American television. Networks do not yet feel that a wide enough sector of the country would tune in to such showcases.

Cable television now transmits NHL games to homes throughout the southern half of the United States. For most residents of that region, though, hockey rules and strategy remain clouded in mystery. In addition, many first-time spectators at NHL games, well-versed in other sports, feel too embarrassed to ask friends or fans in adjoining seats the elementary questions necessary to understand and enjoy hockey.

Making matters worse, no inexpensive, comprehensive yet easy-to-follow work has been marketed nationally or internationally, describing how to watch ice hockey. Surely, such a primer could act as an important aid to the interested but untrained fan. Without a steady influx of new ticket buyers, the sport's growth will grind to a halt.

Several excellent biographical works on stars have made bestseller lists and dozens of talented journalists cover NHL teams on almost a daily basis, during the season. Hockey magazines, promotional guides and newspapers overflow with statistics, bits of trivia and player profiles. Occasional articles in newspapers and in NHL team programs and infrequent spots between periods of television hockey broadcasts have been geared toward the hockey dilettante.

Few recent books offer basic descriptions of the

league's format or the game's rules, equipment, shots, strategy and team composition. Millions of potential spectators might well cross over from other sports if they understood better when, and about what, to cheer or boo.

Picture yourself as so unfamiliar with football that the only parts of the game you enjoy are scores and fights. Stand in the shoes of a baseball neophyte whose only thrill comes on the rare moments when a slugger belts a home run. For the rest of the time, especially during games when one team jumps out to a sizable lead, you'd feel bored stiff.

If you have a similar sensation at a hockey game, appreciating only the goals or the rumbles, if you feel befuddled by the difference between icing and offsides, if you don't know a forward from a defenseman, this book is for you. If you grew up around ice hockey, or are one of the 11.5 million fans who attend NHL games annually, this handbook can fill the gaps in your knowledge and can answer some of the questions you've always had about the sport.

Chapter One
Game and League Format and a Player Profile

On December 19th, 1917, in the midst of World War I, the NHL embarked on its maiden season, with only four teams. In almost 70 years since its creation, the NHL has grown to 21 teams and split into two conferences, each of which includes two divisions. Teams within divisions play 35 of their 80 regular-season games in their own division. Therefore, to cut down on transportation costs, divisions are composed of teams from the same general, geographic regions.

The Prince of Wales Conference comprises both the six-team Patrick Division (Philadelphia Flyers, Washington Capitals, New York Islanders, New York Rangers, Pittsburgh Penguins, New Jersey Devils) and the five-team Adams Division (Quebec Nordiques, Montreal Canadiens, Buffalo Sabres, Boston Bruins, Hartford Whalers). The Clarence Campbell Conference includes the Norris Division (St. Louis Blues, Chicago Black Hawks, Minnesota North Stars, Detroit Red Wings, Toronto Maple Leafs) and the Smythe Division (Edmonton Oilers, Winnipeg Jets, Calgary Flames Los Angeles Kings, Vancouver Canucks).

Each league member plays 40 games at home and 40 on the road during the regular season. The top four finishers in each division, or 16 of the 21 teams, make the playoffs, which start in April, at the end of the regular season.

NHL hockey games, won by the squad scoring the most goals, are divided into three, 20-minute periods, which

9

take between two and three hours to complete. Intermissions between periods supposedly last 15 minutes, but now with TV coverage, may stretch beyond that time limit.

Each team is allowed one 30-second time-out during regulation or in an overtime of a playoff game. The time-out, which usually is called near the end of the third period, must be taken during a regular stoppage of play. Any player designated by the coach may indicate to the referee that his team wants a time-out.

Tied games are followed by a two-minute rest period during which players remain on the ice. After this pause, a five-minute, sudden-death overtime takes place to break the deadlock. If no team scores, the game ends in a tie, except in playoff competition, when additional overtimes are added.

When a game ends tied during the playoffs, players receive a 15-minute break before the 20-minute, sudden-death overtime. If that overtime ends tied, another period is added until one team scores to break the deadlock. During the interval between the overtime periods, teams return to the dressing rooms and the ice is flooded, shaved and smoothed.

For every win chalked up, teams receive two points. Ties result in one point and losers get none. The four leaders in point total from each division advance to the playoff quest for the Stanley Cup, the sport's Super Bowl, held in the end of May. Procedures similar to those in other professional sports resolve ties in the standings and determine seedings and matchups in the tournament.

Three-out-of-five-game series open the first round of the playoffs. From that point on, four-out-of-seven-game battles take place. Depending on how their team fares, each player may earn from $2,000 (if they lose in the first round) to $20,000 during the playoffs.

Twenty players from each team dress for NHL hockey games. Of the 18 forwards and defensemen and two goaltenders, only six squad members can take the ice as a unit. Those six include the goalie, two defensemen and three forwards (right wing, left wing and center).

NHL Player Profile

From what countries do NHL players originate? The league has truly achieved an international flavor over the last 20 years. As of October 16, 1984, 399 or 76.6% of the league's 521 players were Canadian, 63 or 12.1% were American born (compared with six during the 1967-68 season), 57 or 10.9% were European and two players came from elsewhere. Of the Europeans, 28 were Swedish, 13 Czechoslovakian, 11 Finnish, two West German. France, Switzerland and Yugoslavia each had one representative.

According to Gary Meagher, assistant director of information for the NHL, the typical league player is 6-feet tall, 25.7 years old and weighs 189 pounds. On average, these chosen few from among the ranks of millions of amateurs, last 4.5 years in the pros.

Canadians generally come up and win a scout's notice through their well-organized, national junior-league system, which includes the Western, Ontario and the Quebec Hockey Leagues. According to Bob McKenzie writing in *The Hockey News*, "Nineteen of the top 21 prospects available for the 1985 draft—according to the NHL Central Scouting Bureaus's so-called confidential ratings list—are playing in either the Western or Ontario Leagues."

McKenzie continues, "In the past couple of drafts, major junior hockey's development efforts have been overshadowed by those of U.S. high schools and colleges, as well as European leagues. But this year, the U.S. high schoolers and Europeans are nowhere to be found. And while that, as much as anything else, reflects the cyclical nature of the entry draft, junior hockey operators who have been put on the defensive aren't about to let this slide by unnoticed."

"I've noticed in the last little while a renewed sense of

enthusiasm for our product," gushed Ontario Hockey League Commissioner and Canadian Major Junior Hockey League executive David Branch. "I think it started with our gold medal win at the world junior championships in Helsinki and now the NHL is showing some interest in revamping the (draft) system that has hurt our product over the years."

As recently as 10 years ago, players were never drafted before their 20th birthday. Now, most Canadian blue-chip prospects have been selected before reaching 18 years of age. Canadian students picked during college years can try out in NHL training camps without fear of losing remaining collegiate eligibility. Once offered a contract, a player may either accept it or turn it down, and still return to his university squad.

But National Collegiate Athletic Association (NCAA) rules regarding members of American university teams differ significantly from those adhered to in Canada. Mere attendance at an NHL training camp forces loss of future collegiate eligibility under NCAA rules. Players from American universities, whether Canadian nationals or not, must feel sure of making an NHL club's roster or face a substantial risk. For that reason, Americans entering the NHL are generally older than Canadian rookies.

Chapter Two

Where to Sit, Programs and the Rink

The Best Seats in the House

Inexperienced fans frequently purchase seats directly behind a team bench, believing them ideal spots to watch a game. Certainly you can get a close-up view of players crashing into the boards and checking one another. But if you want to hear a coach's instructions to his squad or get an entire picture of the rink as plays develop, you will have made a poor choice.

The scratched-up plexiglass tends to muffle sound, preventing a coach's voice from reaching the stands and tending to obstruct a clear view of the action. Far better spots to view the action of a hockey game lay half way up the stands and toward one end of the rink. From those locations, fans can see the entire rink area and can watch plays as they develop. Scouts usually sit in these areas, as do retired players, injured team members and active reserves.

Tickets may cost anywhere from $8 to $25, depending on the city and the location of the seat. Multigame packages or season tickets may or may not reduce the price per game, but can guarantee playoff tickets in an ideal position to spectate.

Programs

Programs purchased before the game provide detailed lineups of both teams and include articles describing player backgrounds, current transactions, team statistics and bits of trivia. Players from both rosters are listed by position and number. Statistics indicate games played, goals scored, assists made, total points (which combines these last two factors) and penalty minutes. Goalie records are also displayed.

Notice also a column showing a + or - rating. This figure indicates how many goals were scored by a player's team (when short-handed or at equal strength, not on power plays) while he was on the ice, less how many goals the opposition tallied during that time. If because of a penalty a team is short-handed and is scored upon, the plus-minus rating of the members of the scored-upon team is unaffected.

A high positive number indicates a good offensive output and tough defense, a figure carefully scrutinized by the management. Wayne Gretzky, Edmonton's superstar forward, had an incredible plus 76 rating during the 1983-84 regular season, during which he accounted for 87 goals and 118 assists.

goals for - goals against = plus or minus rating.
Gretzky won the Emory Edge Award for top plus-minus rating in 1985, and was the NHL's player of the year.

Generally, programs include brief explanations of basic hockey rules and may contain a page on which fans can keep track of the game's action. After each period the press is given a similar, filled-out score sheet which lists individual shots on goal, goal scorers, who assisted, who was on the ice during the goal, and the time of the score (figure 1).

Figure 1. An example of a score sheet, before it's been filled out and given to the press.

OFFICIAL SCORESHEET

DATE _____

REFEREE _____

LINESMEN _____

SCORE					
TEAM	1	2	3	*OT	T

SHOTS ON GOAL					
TEAM	1	2	3	*OT	T

OPPONENTS STARTING LINEUP
GOAL
D
D
LW
C
RW
Back-Up Goalie
Other Defense Pairs:
Other Forward Lines:
Spares:

HOME TEAM STARTING LINEUP
GOAL
D
D
LW
C
RW
Back-Up Goalie
Other Defense Pairs:
Other Forward Lines:
Spares:

GOALS SCORED

PLAYER	TEAM	PER.	TIME	ASSISTS

PENALTY RECORD

PLAYER	TEAM	PER.	OFF	ON	MIN	PENALTY

The Rink

Official NHL hockey rinks are 200-feet long and 85-feet wide (figure 2). Corners are rounded in the arc of a circle with a radius of 28 feet. Some older rinks, like Boston Garden (195' x 83') and Chicago Stadium (188' x 85'), have perimeter measurements slightly smaller than these dimensions.

Wood or fiberglass walls (**boards**) rise between 40 and 48 inches (ideally 42) above the ice surface. Aside from official markings, the playing surface and boards are colored white. The kick plate below the board, made out of hard plastic, is light blue or yellow.

Attached above the boards is an almost unbreakable plexiglass rim, designed to help prevent pucks from flying into the stands. Notice the glass stands much higher behind the goals than along the sides of the rink. This additional barrier has three functions: protecting the fans in the areas of the rinks where pucks are most often shot, providing a soundproofing effect for players on the ice, and shielding team members from rowdy fans who have been known to throw beer or take punches at skaters.

Goalposts and Nets

The **goalposts** and **nets** stand 10 feet from each end of the rink and in the center of a two-inch-wide, red **goal line** which runs the width of the ice and continues up the boards. Horizontal posts are set six feet apart and vertical posts extend four feet above the ice surface.

A crossbar extends between the tops of both vertical posts and the goalposts. Both the goalposts and the crossbars are painted red and other exterior surfaces white. Foam rubber surrounds the rimming to aid in limiting injury. The goal's tough net is made of nylon.

Figure 2. This illustration displays official NHL rink.

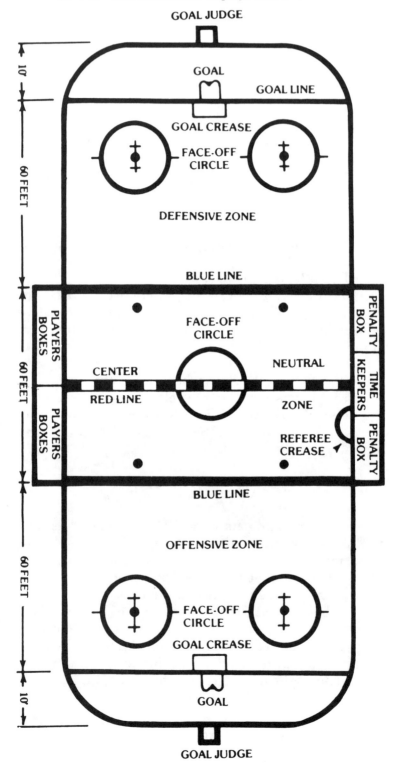

The Goal Line and Pucks

The **goal line** has two important functions. One of those involves icing, described in detail in Chapter Seven. For shots to count as goals, pucks must completely cross the red goal line. **Pucks** are vulcanized rubber disks with bevelled edges. These tiny missiles have home-team emblems embossed on one side. They are one-inch thick, three inches in diameter and weigh 5.5 to six ounces, according to NHL rules (figure 3).

Between games pucks are kept in a freezer. During games pucks are immersed in an ice and brine solution, to keep them at a temperature below freezing. This process prevents pucks from bouncing, making them easier to pass and stickhandle.

Figure 3. **This collection of pucks represents 18 present and past (Oakland Seals, Kansas City Scouts and Atlanta Flames) NHL teams.**

The Goal Crease

The **goal crease** is the rectangular area marked by a two-inch-wide red line in front of each goal. Unless pushed, if an opposing player stands in the crease and a goal is scored by one of his teammates, that score will not count.

However, a goal is allowed if a player inside the crease makes the shot himself. One other rule pertaining to this area is that players can not hit the goaltender when he stands in the crease. Some officials, though, have been known to overlook violations of this tenet.

Ice-Surface Division

Since introduced by Lester and Frank Patrick in 1918, the ice area between the two goals has been split into three zones by two, one-foot-wide **blue lines,** drawn 60 feet out and parallel to the goal lines at both ends of the rink. Linesmen straddle these lines to position themselves to make offsides calls.

One of the three areas delineated by these blue lines is the **defending zone,** the territory closest to a team's goal. The defensive zone for one team forms the **attack zone** for the other, and vice versa. The central portion of the rink, between the two blue lines, composes the **neutral zone.**

Another term hockey fans should recognize is **"the point."** The unmarked point area is near the left or right boards, just inside the opposing team's blue line. Frequently, defensemen occupy these slots and either feed passes to teammates or shoot the puck hard and low, hoping for a deflection. The point is a good place to shoot from since the goaltender's vision is often screened by players battling in front of him.

The 12-inch-wide, red **center line** also runs parallel to the goal lines and is painted in center ice. Regulation lines contain uniform, distinctive designs at regular intervals, making them easily distinguishable from blue lines.

Center-Ice Spot and Circle

A 12-inch-diameter, circular blue spot painted in the rink's center marks the center of a blue circle 15 feet in radius, where the game's opening face-off takes place. Face-offs also occur here to start each period, after every goal and following an incorrect call by a referee or linesman. A puck will also be placed on the dot just before a penalty shot is taken.

Face-Off Spots in the Neutral Zone

Notice the four, red, two-foot-diameter dots at each end of the neutral zone, five feet from each blue line and 44 feet apart. Face-offs due to offsides infractions will generally occur at one of the dots, just outside of the blue lines.

End-Zone Face-Off Spots and Circles

In both end zones and on both sides of each goal, red face-off spots lay in the center of four, large face-off circles, with 15-foot radii. When a goaltender smothers a puck, a face-off takes place in one of these areas.

The dots are where the two opposing forwards stand with their sticks on the ice, ready to attack the puck when dropped. Each teams' forwards stand with their backs to their goalies.

These face-off circles come within 10 feet of the net and are 40 feet away from the goal line at their farthest end. They act as perfect locations for goal scoring. Pucks can easily be passed to players waiting in "the slot," the area between the face-off circles and 20 feet from the net.

High-velocity, straight-on shots on goal can be made from the slot.

Player and Penalty Benches

Along the ice in the neutral zone, as close to the rink's center as possible, are the players' benches. The 24-foot-long benches must accomodate at least 14 people. Penalty benches are also situated in the neutral zone, usually on the opposite side of the rink from the player benches.

But in venues where team benches are on opposite sides of the stands, as in Montreal, the penalty box adjoins the home-team area. This alignment provides an advantage to the Canadiens, who have only 10 feet to go to return from the penalty box to their bench. Visitors, on the other hand, must skate all the way across the ice, 85 feet, to reach their bench.

Chapter Three

Team Positions

The 20 players from each team who dress for an NHL hockey game include 18 forwards and defensemen and two goaltenders. Only six members of each squad can take the ice at one time: one goaltender, two defensemen and three forwards (right wing, left wing and center).

Two goalkeepers are necessary in case the starting goalie is hurt. In that event, the substitute goaltender may enter the game, but according to the rules, no warm-up is permitted. Occasionally this rule has not been enforced. If both listed nettenders are hurt, teams may insert any eliglible goalkeeper, who then receives two minutes to loosen up.

Each club appoints one team captain. In principle, he is the only one on the ice allowed to question calls made by a referee. The captain wears a 3-inch-high "C" on the front of his sweater. No playing coach, manager or goaltender may act as captain.

Defensemen

Usually, rosters contain three pairs of defensemen, one of which takes the ice at any given time. Although some small, shifty types have been successful in this position, defensemen, typically, are built tall and strong.

Defensemen excel at backward skating, which they do about 60% of their time on the ice and drill into their systems through constant repetition in practice. They must anticipate their competitor's plays and passes and break up attacks, either by stealing the puck or by administering crisp body checks. In addition, they try to clear their own net of aggressive forwards, allowing their goaltender unimpeded views of incoming pucks.

As mentioned earlier, in an offensive scheme, defensemen generally stay back at the point. From those perimeters, they may snap crisp, direct passes to forwards or wind up and blast slap shots, which may reach velocities of 120 miles per hour. On **slap shots,** in some ways similar to golf swings, players raise sticks to shoulder height and accelerate them down at the puck, finishing with a full follow through.

Today, most defensemen no longer function solely as intimidators and concentrate much more on offense than did their predecessors. One of many exceptions to this rule is 6-foot-3, 215-pound Rod Langway of the Washington Capitals, a tough-hitting, defensive standout willing to sacrifice his body to halt the puck's advance (figure 4). Langway, cut in the mold of former prototypes at his position, won the Norris Trophy as best defenseman in the NHL during both the 1982-83 and 1983-84 seasons.

But many other active all-star defensemen possess passing and shooting skills never dreamed of 20 years ago. The New York Islander's Denis Potvin had more assists (25) than any player in playoff history, prior to 1985. Edmonton's swift-skating defensemen, Paul Coffey, was runner-up to Wayne Gretzky for the scoring title in 1983-84 with 126 points, including 40 goals. During the 1984-85 regular season, he finished fifth in scoring with 121 points. In the 1985 playoffs, he set Stanley Cup records for goals, assists and points by a defenseman (figure 5). Montreal's Larry Robinson, MVP in the 1978 playoffs, is another example of a defenseman who can score with ease.

The revolution in the style of the well-known stars active as defensemen can be traced back to the emerg-

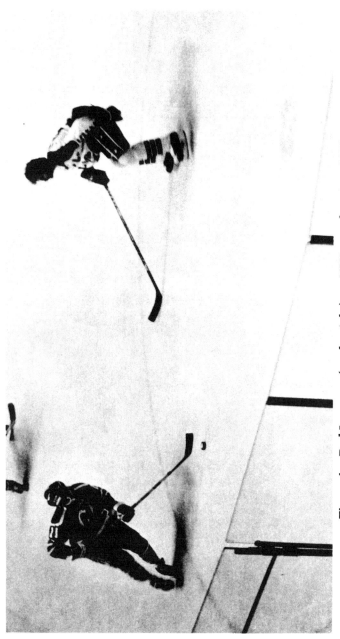

Figure 4. Rod Langway (on the right), an NHL member since 1978, was traded by Montreal to Washington in 1982. Langway remains one of the few active veterans who plays without a helmet, a privilege granted to those who entered the league before 1979.

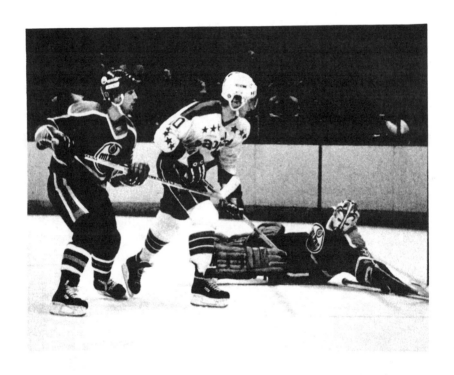

Figure 5. Edmonton Oiler Paul Coffey (at left), the 1985 Norris Trophy winner as best defenseman, appears to hook the Capital's Bobby Carpenter. Goaltender Grant Fuhr desperately scrambles to cover up. Although apparently guilty of an infraction here, the swift-skating Coffey has been a stellar performer for his team since joining the NHL during the 1980-81 season. Photo by J. Henson Photographics.

ence of the Boston Bruins' incomparable Bobby Orr. In the late 1960s and 1970s, Orr opened up new vistas at this position by utilizing his spectacular skating and stickhandling abilities to rack up goals at a previously unmatched pace. In both 1970-71 and 1974-75 Orr, who played on two Stanley-Cup-champion teams, led the league in scoring. As Wayne Gretzky does now, Orr could control the flow of a game and determine its outcome.

Before the Orr era, with few exceptions, defensemen did little more than hindering an opponent's rushes or making short passes to forwards. Orr, an eight-time winner of the Norris trophy, not only revamped the role of the defenseman, but through his friend and agent, Toronto attorney Alan Eagleson, almost singlehandedly changed the NHL's salary structure.

In 1966, Eagleson negotiated a two-year, $40,000-per-season contract for his rookie client, more than quadrupling the previous norm for a first-year, NHL regular. With players flocking to him for counsel, Eagleson led the drive to organize the NHL Players Association, and organized the 1972 Team Canada-USSR series that introduced the NHL to international hockey.

Some hockey aficionados complain that because of Orr's influence, youngsters have lost the art of playing defense. During the 1980-1981 season for example, the league's 21 teams averaged 3.85 goals per game, the highest mark since the NHL introduced the center red line in 1943.

Several explanations have been proposed for this new trend. Increased use of the slap shot, teams' growing reliance on backup goaltenders and the replacement of older veterans with faster, more-aggressive young players certainly have contributed to the goal rush.

Perhaps most important is that American audiences, nurtured on high-scoring basketball and football games, prefer offensive displays to low-scoring defensive struggles. Recent NFL teams have chalked up record numbers of points. In the 1984-85 season, quarterback Dan Marino of the Miami Dolphins shattered long-held marks by midseason. Edmonton Oiler superstar, Gretzky, summed the situation up saying, "Fans like to see 6-5 games more than 1-0 games. I know I prefer them, too."

Forwards

NHL teams usually dress four forward lines (left and right wings and a center), totalling 12 players. Coaches look for balance in deciding which three skaters to pair together on a forward line. One such trio might consist of a playmaking, high-scoring center, one offensive-minded wing, and one defense-oriented wing.

An example of such a combination where the elements gelled to perfection was the Boston Bruin line of 1970-71, which included center Phil Esposito and wings Ken Hodge and Wayne Cashman. These three set a league scoring record. Esposito totaled 76 goals and the same number of assists. Hodge scored 43 times and Cashman, a defensive standout and great passer, added 21 goals (figure 6).

Wings, as their name implies, skate up and down the rink, usually staying fairly close to the boards, stationed on the sides, like wide receivers in football. On defense, wings generally check their counterpart opponents and try to thwart their attacks on goal. When a puck enters their defensive zone, wings should still remain a bit conservative, keeping their distance from their own goal. They must always be ready to reverse direction in case their defense steals the puck and then starts its own rush.

Bobby Hull (left wing), Mike Bossy and Mike Gartner (right wing) are three role models for young, aspiring skaters. Hull, the "Golden Jet" of the Chicago Black Hawks, led the NHL in goals seven times, and three times took honors as the overall point-scoring titlist. Hull, a gregarious good-will ambassador, accounted for 610 goals in his 1,063-game career.

The 6-foot-tall, 185-pound Bossy, of the New York

Figure 6. In this vintage photograph, Boston's Wayne Cashman (on the right) and Montreal's hall-of-fame goaltender, Ken Dryden, battle for the loose puck as referee Bob Myers observes. Photo by Denis Brodeur.

Islanders, an incredibly accurate shooter and master of the quick release, had accounted for 416 goals and 811 points in his 533 NHL games prior to the 1984-85 season (figure 7). "The Boss" amassed 58 goals and 59 assists for 117 points during 1984-85, and set the mark as the first player to hit the 50-goal plateau in his initial eight years in the league. His 81 playoff goals put him one behind Maurice "The Rocket" Richard for most scores in the playoffs.

Montreal's Richard remains the all-time leader in career playoff hat tricks with seven. A **hat trick** may be defined as three goals by the same player in the same game. A **"pure" hat trick** occurs when one player scores three consecutive goals.

Gartner, the articulate, all-time leader for the Washington Capitals in career goals, assists, points and games, is a right-handed shot and a natural right winger. He defines his offensive job as "shooting the puck as much as possible. From the red line in, I'm looking to get myself into an opening."

"Defensively, when the puck is on my side of the ice, I'm checking the opposition point man. When the puck is in the opposite corner, I'm covering the slot. Wings play zone rather than man-to-man defense," explains Gartner, the first Washington Capital to reach the 500-point plateau, capping his 50-goal, 102-point 1984-85 year (figure 8).

How does a wing determine when to go with a slap shot or a far more streamlined wrist shot? According to Gartner, "The more time you have, the more opportunity to take a slap shot. When you're in a tight situation, close in to the net, a wrist shot is called for. Ninety percent of the time, a wrist shot is the one used."

Gartner says he doesn't think the Capitals will ever evoke the type of fan enthusiasm generated by the Redskins. But, he adds, "Our popularity is growing and will continue to improve as long as we perform well. Now that we are winning, more and more younger kids are

Figure 7. High-scoring Mike Bossy unleashes a drive on Washington's Pat Riggin, who has come out to cut the angle down perfectly.

31

**Figure 8.   Mike Gartner's 50th goal of the 1984-85 season was cap-
tured in this spectacular action shot. The Ontario native reached his
career high on this score against the Pittsburgh Penguins.** Photo by J.
Henson Photographics.

getting into junior hockey in our area. Once they become involved, they get their parents to bring them to games, creating a domino-type effect (figure 9)."

Centermen

Unlike wings, centermen roam throughout the attack zone, scrambling to set up and create offensive opportunities. Skaters at this glamorous position have much in common with playmaking point guards in basketball. Good centers are adept skaters, accurate shooters and must be strong, tough and fearless.

Often the team leader in point totals, centers reap in publicity as well as money. Frequently, centers are shorter and lighter than wingers, who must do more bruising in the corners to control loose pucks.

Many experts believe Wayne Gretzky is the greatest hockey player of all time (figure 10). The phenomenal center maximizes his formidable skills and almost daily mesmerizes both his opponents and the fans. His presence almost guarantees a sellout for the host club.

Gretzky's gifts include phenomenal anticipation of the movements of his teammates and of the puck, a dead-eye shot, superb reflexes and the wisdom to know his limitations. Like Larry Bird of the NBA Boston Celtics, he may not be the league's best athlete. He is nonetheless, without doubt, the NHL's most valuable player and its best draw. Both Gretzky and Bird have the imagination and skill to regularly create shots and passes that amaze opponents, fans and commentators.

New York Rangers defensemen and team captain, Barry "Bubba" Beck, has said of Gretzky, "He's like a great wide receiver. He always finds the open spot. His first three or four strides are very quick, although he's not that fast overall." As soon as one of his teammates touches the puck on defense, Gretzky shoots down the ice leading the Oilers fast-break offense.

"Every time we play against him," added the burly,

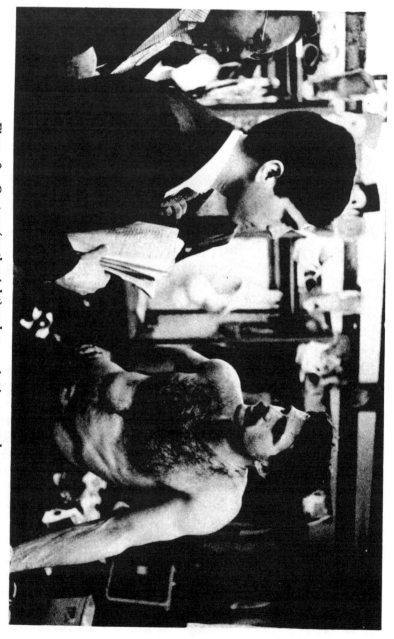

Figure 9. Gartner (on the right) makes a point in a casual postgame interview with author Mitch Henkin.

Figure 10. Wayne Gretzky at work. AP/Wide World Photo.

6-foot-3 215-pound Beck, "I'll see another move or two that I've never seen anyone do before. The next day, I'll try it in practice and it never looks as good."

How great is the great Gretzky, the *Sporting News* 1984-85 NHL player of the year for an unprecedented fifth straight year? The 6-foot-tall, 170-pound center won the Hart trophy as the league's MVP six straight years from 1979 to 1985, tying Gordie Howe for most awards in that category. Gretzky captained his first Stanley-Cup-winning team at the age of 23 and has averaged almost a goal a game the last four years.

He was named 1985 Conn Smythe Trophy-winner (playoff MVP), leading his Oilers to their second consecutive Stanley Cup, and third straight appearance in the finals. Also during the 1984-85 season, he led the NHL with 73 goals and 135 assists for 208 points.

He holds about 40 NHL records, including most assists, and through all of his success, has remained gracious and accessible. Gretzky turned pro for the old World Hockey Association's Indianapolis Racers when he was 17. He earns about two million dollars a year, not bad for a high school dropout.

Goaltenders

Goaltenders, who may have the biggest hearts on the squad, are usually the least burly players on the team. Still, no prerequisite height or weight determines success at this crucial position. Ken Dryden of the Montreal Canadiens, the NHL's most-famous goalie during the 1970s, was 6-foot-4, 220 pounds (figure 11). Dryden, out of Cornell University, is the Ivy League's most successful representative in the NHL. He led the way for American college players aspiring to careers in the league.

Dryden, who now works with the Ontario provincial government, says he chose Cornell because he never thought of hockey as a career. Dryden dominated NCAA hockey during his tenure, leaving with a 1.67 average and

Figure 11. **The remarkable Ken Dryden stretches all 6-foot-4 to stop this Chicago Black Hawk forward.** Photo by Denis Brodeur.

one loss in his three years of varsity hockey.

After graduating in 1969, he was called up to play with the Canadiens in the playoffs after the 1970-71 season. His performance for the Stanley Cup champions won him the Conn Smythe award as playoff MVP, an incredible feat for a first-year goaltender.

Goaltenders act as the last line of defense. The phrase, "The buck stops here," literally applies to his job and import on the ice. When a team's fortunes rise, goalies bask in praise. On the contrary, when a club's record tumbles, goaltenders may receive disproportionate amounts of blame.

The solitary goal protector must have the reflexes of a karate black belt, skate backwards as well as a defenseman, possess great flexibility and use enough muscle to prevent getting bullied around. He can spark a deflated squad with a super save, or reverse positive momentum with a brief lapse in concentration. Not the least of his problems is to maintain his psychological equilibrium when taken on the roller-coaster ride of support of both the fans and the media.

An intelligent pitcher has a mental book on what pitches to throw at certain batters and must know a hitter's strengths and vulnerabilities. So also must goaltenders study opponents and anticipate their reactions in various situations. Will the attacking player take a slap shot, pass, go low or high or try to deek, a fake accomplished by moving the puck from the forehand part of the stick to the backhand?

Even the most talented NFL quarterbacks serve a five-year apprenticeship before learning how to properly read defenses and react to changing defensive alignments. The NHL goalie faces an equally difficult task.

From Montreal's Jacques Plante (the first goaltender to wear a mask) to Chicago's Glen Hall (who played more consecutive games than any other goalie) to Ken Dryden, goaltenders have been the bulwark of championship teams. Winning the World Series requires great pitching.

The Super Bowl champs always have had a quarterback at the helm who could remain cool under pressure and motivate their team through their leadership. Similarly, the Stanley Cup's outcome often rests squarely on the solitary goaltender's shoulders. Goaltenders are so valuable to their teams, that a whole chapter has been devoted to the position later on.

Chapter Four

Equipment

Retail cost for outfits worn by forwards and defense-men vary from $250 to $700. The goalie's armour-like suit costs even more. Of course, from the junior and college ranks up, players get their equipment for free. These lucky ones don't have to worry about equipment expense. However, for youths entering the sport, the initial investment can be sizable. Let's start at the bottom of the wardrobe and work our way up.

Skate Blades and Boots

All skates share one feature: they must all be equipped with approved, safety heel tips. Although the stainless-steel skate blades of forwards, defenseman and goaltenders may, at first glance, look the same, each has a subtle but significantly different shape (figure 12).

Forwards' blades are designed so that as little of the blade as possible touches the ice, allowing those players to skate, shift direction and maneuver quickly. The defenseman's blade is flatter or less curved than that of the forward, providing less speed but added stability. Nearly the whole blade of the goaltender's skate rests on the ice surface, yielding speed with less effort. The additional bars above the blade prevent pucks from slipping through the blade and the skate boot.

Blades of forwards are sharpened daily (figure 13), providing a firmer grip on the ice and allowing for clean-

Figure 12.   The left skate belongs to a goaltender. Notice the limited space between the blade and the boot, which prevents pucks from slipping through. The right skate is that of a defenseman or forward. The blade is made of stainless steel.

Figure 13.   In a few minutes, skates can be sharpened on this machine.

er turns and less slips. Blades are wiped dry after every practice or game.

Hockey boots may either be stitched (leather and nylon) or more commonly molded (hard plastic) for added protection. The goaltender's skate has thick rubber padding around the toe and some defensemen use extra protection around their ankles and the skate's instep.

Shin Guards, Hockey Pants, Shoulder and Elbow Pads and Sweaters

Shin guards or pads run from the center of the knee to about one inch above the foot, where the boot begins (figure 14). The forwards' fiberglass, felt-lined shin pads are smaller, not as bulky and cover less of the knee than those of defensemen, who block more shots. Sometimes players line the inside of these pads with cotton to add insulation, before putting them against their legs. Shin pads are covered with the team's hockey socks, and are kept in place by tight tape over the socks.

Goaltenders don't wear shin pads underneath their socks but rather put goaltending pads over the sock tops (figure 15). These leather pads are lined with horse or deer hair and with absorbed perspiration in the late stages of the game, can easily weigh 25 to 30 pounds.

Above and over the shin pads and held up by suspenders are nylon hockey pants padded at the hips, seat and thighs (figure 16). Forwards' and defensemen's pant pads are rounded while those of the goalie are flat, preventing pucks from ricocheting sideways and making them pop straight up.

Continuing up the body, players don shoulder and elbow pads. Slip-on or velcro-closing elbow pads provide essential protection for this vulnerable area. Some defensemen wear more cumbersome elbow pads than shooter-oriented forwards who don't want their arm movement restricted.

43

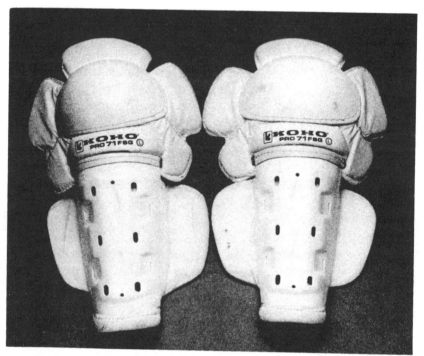

Figure 14. Defensemen and forwards wear shin pads like these under the team's hockey socks.

Shoulder pads, protected with heavy plastic and including adjustable, elastic straps, come down from the top of the shoulders over the upper arms to below the breast area (figure 17). A defenseman's pad may extend over the abdomen, if that player blocks lots of shots.

The goaltender's made-to-measure, chest protector looks like a baseball umpire's jacket and functions in a similar manner. This breast plate, which can become very heavy when soaked with sweat, covers the upper body with either heavy plastic or thick cotton padding.

Over their shoulder pads, all skaters wear nylon sweaters, which don't absorb sweat but do ventilate well. Each player's name adorns the back of his sweater, at shoulder height, in block letters three inches high. Identifying numbers at least 10 inches high are sewn in under the names. White sweaters are worn at home and dark-colored ones are used on the road.

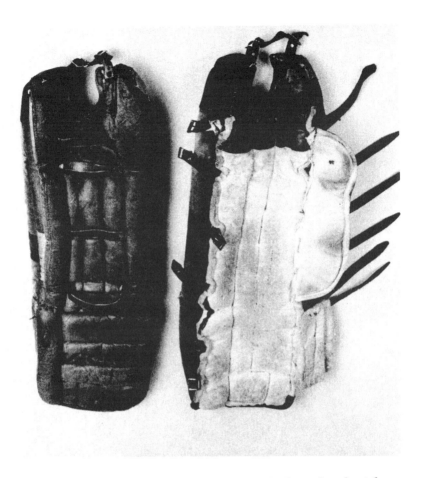

Figure 15.   On the left is the goalie's left leg pad. The pad on the right was included to show the felt lining that holds the straps and fill in place.

Although hockey helmets have been available for 90 years, they were seldom used until the last decade. Now, for all NHL professionals who signed contracts after 1979, today's vastly improved models are required. The helmet's tough outer shell must withstand 20 foot pounds of pressure and must resist cracks and blade penetration. Special padding inside helps absorb and distribute shock.

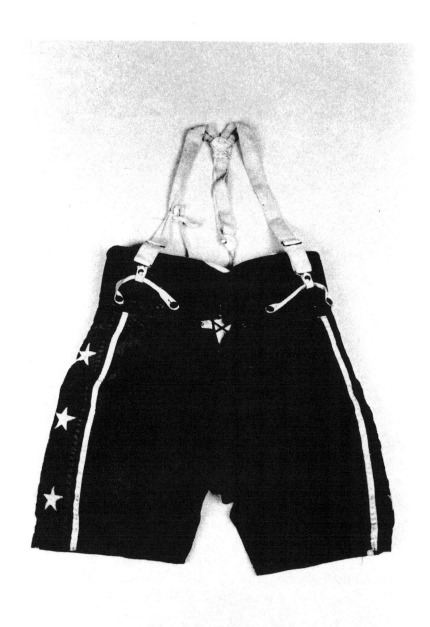

Figure 16. Hockey pants, whose color varies according to the team's color scheme, are made of nylon with pads sewn into the interior.

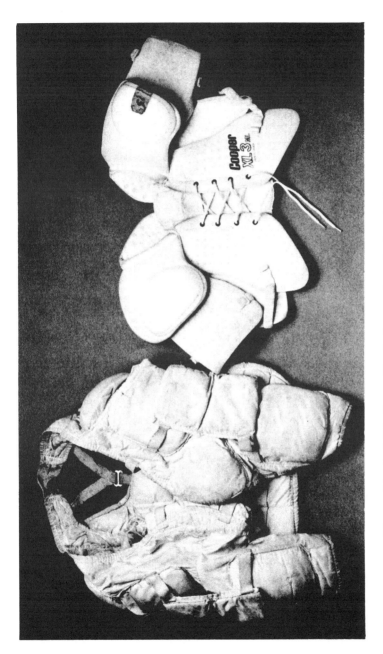

Figure 17. At left is the goaltender's one-piece chest protector, arm and elbow pads. At right is the shoulder pad typically worn by defensemen and forwards.

Face protectors, mandatory at the junior level, have helped prevent serious eye injury and will allow more and more future hockey players to go through their careers without ever losing a tooth. When today's juniors reach the pro ranks, these protectors may become commonplace.

These masks can be clear plastic visors (which like racquetball and ski goggles, may fog up) polycarbonate visors (which can react with vinyl car seats to produce stress fractures) or wire cages (whose bars may restrict vision). The tradeoff of improved safety for slightly reduced visibility has been accepted in many sports today.

Several years ago, many goalies wore solid, molded-fiberglass masks. But since these masks fit so closely to the face, when the puck hit around one of the openings, the mask would dig into the skin, causing bad cuts. Now, most goaltenders put on cage-type masks with the cage constructed away from the face. This protection holds in heat and impairs vision somewhat, but again the safety factor outweighs these difficulties. Goalies at all levels of play wear some type of mask (figure 18).

Most forwards and defensemen use mouth protectors. Goaltenders do not, since they must constantly shout instructions to teammates. In addition, the wire cages keep pucks away from the goaltender's teeth.

Gloves

Forwards and defensemen may select either leather gloves or nylon ones with leather palms. Both varieties allow individual finger movement and attempt to prevent blade slashes by utilizing pads to protect the thumb, fingers, back of the hand and wrist.

Unlike their teammates, goalies wear two different gloves on their hands. On his stick hand, the goaltender has a flat fiberglass and leather **"blocker,"** molded in the fashion of a Middle-Age-warrior's shield. Behind the flat shield lays the glove, with individual spaces for fingers and thick padding surrounding the thumb.

The goaltender's other **"trapper"** glove, parallels the look and webbing of a first-baseman's mitt in baseball. This glove, heavily padded near the fatty part of the thumb, allows goalies to catch pucks, and helps in preventing serious bruises (figure 19).

Sticks

Perhaps the most crucial, personalized and pampered piece of the NHL pro's gear is his stick. Sticks, which weigh between 17 and 25 ounces, are made to order to a pro's specifications by manufacturers, just as fine clothiers tailor suits for their clients. The average player may go through 10 dozen sticks a year, at a wholesale cost to the club of $10 each.

Hockey sticks (so called because they were originally all wood), like newer tennis racquets and golf clubs, now come designed in a multitude of colors, weights and lengths. Although most consist, in large part, of wood, other popular ingredients include fiberglass, plastic and graphite.

According to the NHL rulebook, "Adhesive tape of any color may be wrapped around the stick at any place for the purpose of reinforcement or to improve control of the puck." All sticks, including the goalie's, must be 58 inches or less in length (55 inches is about average) from heel to the end of the shaft and can measure no more than 12.5 inches from the heel to the end of the blade. The stick's blade must measure between two and three inches in width.

Some players alter the length of their sticks as the season progresses. Wayne Gretzky, for example, told Al Strachan of the *Toronto Globe and Mail*, "Earlier in the season, I use a longer stick because you're still a bit out of shape and you're still sometimes behind the play a bit. With a longer stick, you can reach a bit further. I gradually cut off a bit more as the season goes on and by the playoffs, I'm cutting off 4.5 inches."

Figure 18. From left to right, the most-often-used cage-type goal-tender mask of today, the molded-fiberglass model popular until the early 1980s and one of the helmets worn by all defensemen and forwards who entered the NHL after 1979.

Figure 19. From left to right, a catching glove or trapper worn by a right-handed goaltender, the stick glove (sometimes called the waffle pad) used by a right-handed goalie and the leather glove of forwards and defensemen.

Gretzky, who uses up to 700 sticks a year, or almost three a period, applies black tape to his blade and then rubs on baby powder, accounting for his blade's gray appearance. He feels the powder stops loose ice from adhering to the stick blade. Along with Mike Bossy, he uses one of the heaviest sticks in the league.

The goaltender's stick blade must not exceed 3.5 inches in width, except at the heel, which may be up to 4.5-inches wide. His stick blade must be less than 15.5-inches long, from the heel to the blade's end. Violating these rules results in a minor penalty and a $200 fine.

The curved stick was the brainchild of the Chicago Black Hawks legendary Stan Mikita. As the story goes, Mikita, 7th highest scorer in NHL history with 541 goals in his 1,394 games, took a slap shot in practice and broke his stick. Instead of going over and replacing it, he continued playing with the stick, whose broken blade, by chance, remained in an appropriate curve. To his amazement, Mikita found he shot the puck faster and had an easier time getting it up in the air. Instead of breaking all his sticks, he dipped their shafts in water and used a propane torch to shape the blades' curves.

Now, every NHL team has its own sewing machine (figure 20) and carpentry workshop, stocked with hacksaws, planes, files and blowtorches. Blowtorches are no longer used as frequently, since some newer sticks can't be rebent without impacting on the stick's technical features, while others become brittle after heating.

One consequence of curved sticks is that they make it much more difficult to take backhand shots. Therefore, those shots are used much less frequently than in past times.

Sticks also vary in their **"lies,"** the angle made by the stick's handle and blade. Defensemen generally use more upright sticks with higher lies, where the shaft is straighter to the blade, leading to a smaller blade-to-handle angle. Forwards, who want to keep the puck farther away from their bodies, to shoot with greater velocity, generally select sticks with lower lies or higher blade-to-handle

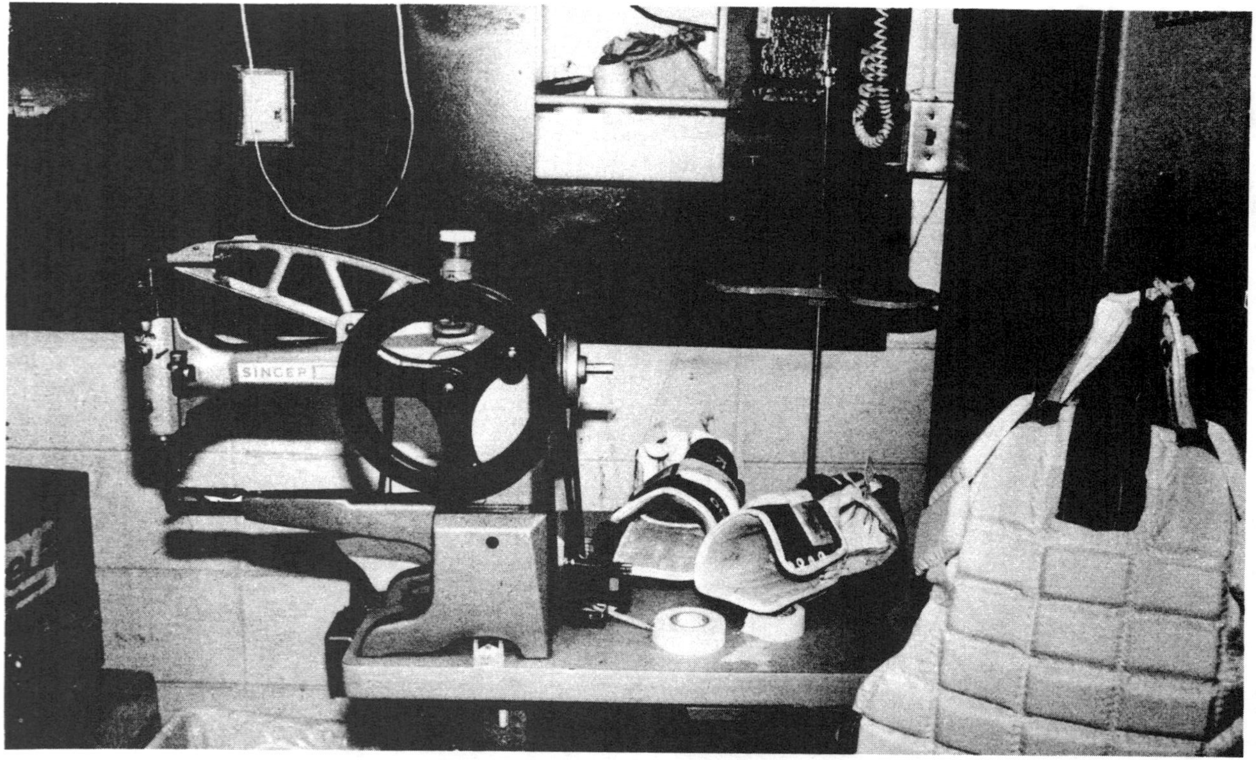

Figure 20. A sewing machine, like this one, is necessary to repair torn equipment.

angles (figure 21).

Righthanders usually put their right hands at the tops of the sticks and shoot from their left sides, while left-handers reverse this procedure. The lower hand is positioned according to the situation. When players **"stickhandle"** (transfer the puck from backhand to forehand and back again), they keep their hands close together, near the top of the stick. But when passing, they move the bottom hand lower. The lower the bottom hand descends, the higher the force of blow achieved. Shooters, therefore, drop that hand down the stick as far as possible.

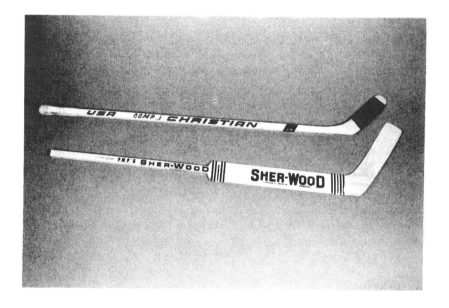

Figure 21. The thinner stick is used by forwards and defensemen. The stick with the wider blade is that of a goaltender.

Chapter Five

Coaches

At a minimum, each NHL team now employs two coaches. This practice grew commonplace after the Russians demonstrated the superiority of the multicoach system during the eight-game series between the select Soviet hockey club and the NHL all-stars in September, 1972.

In the first seven games of that matchup, one of the greatest in the annals of the sport, each team won three times and one game ended tied. In the final game, played in Moscow, Team Canada roared back from a 5-3 deficit, and took the series on Paul Henderson's shot past Vladislav Tretiak. The *Toronto Star*'s Frank Orr branded the game-winner, "the most famous goal in the history of hockey."

Just as NFL assistant coaches sit in the press box and communicate with the head coach on headsets, so does an assistant coach perform that function for NHL clubs. More and more franchises, like the Capitals and the Flyers, also have goaltender coaches, who can relate more easily to the problems involved in that position than can a head coach, who may never have spent a moment in goal.

Warren Strelow, the Washington assistant coach who works with the goalies, helped Herb Brooks with the 1980 U.S. Olympic team. It was Strelow who suggested that Brooks stay with Jim Craig. His faith was justified in Craig, who performed with finesse beyond his years.

Strelow was Brooks' assistant for six years at the University of Minnesota, during which time the Gophers won three NCAA championships. Each of those years, the tournament MVP was a goaltender.

The Capitals signed on Strelow on a one-year, experimental basis in 1983. The two Washington goalies finished first and third in the league that season and had, by far, their best records. Strelow was rewarded with a two-year extension of his contract.

The Caps' General Manager, David Poile, told Robert Fachet of the *Washington Post*, "Our goaltenders have gotten attention that is often overlooked in hockey. Most coaches in preparation for a game discuss forechecking coming out of our end, but never the techniques of goaltending.

"Warren not only works on improving our goaltenders, he also points out the strengths and weaknesses of opposing goaltenders. He works with all the goaltenders in our system and evaluates draftable goaltenders."

Strelow, a netminder at the University of Minnesota as well as with the 1956 Olympic team, told Fachet, "I experience the same feelings as the goaltender. I have a good feeling when they play well, and I share the down side. The goalies often bear the brunt of mistakes made in front of them.

"A goaltender is like a house. Where it's built on a good foundation, you build a goalie on good fundamentals. We do varying drills in practice—drills for movement, reaction drills and game-situation drills. The idea is to do things every day until they become second nature.

In the past, practices centered around shooting and breakouts and special-teams situations. The goalie was just there as a target. That has changed, and I think the results indicate it's for the better."

Head coaches must be multifaceted individuals skilled as teachers, communicators and strategists. They must sense which individuals, when teamed together in lines, achieve the desired chemistry. The ideal head coach establishes a team philosophy, takes part in personnel decisions, makes the right moves at appropriate times during games and acts as guardian to his younger players. He must be forceful enough to discipline veterans who can get out of line.

Good coaches control their emotions and remain cool under the intense pressure and media scrutiny which builds during the season and culminates in the playoff drive. They must instinctively sense how to motivate their charges, without alienating them. They have to forge the team in a certain character, and stick with their gut reactions, even when the team's fortunes ebb.

Bryan Murray joined the Washington organization as head coach in 1981 and in 1984 won the Adams Trophy as NHL coach of the year (figure 22). Before joining the Caps, he was named by *The Hockey News* as Minor League Coach of the year during the 1980-81 season, when he piloted Hershey of the American Hockey League.

Figure 22. Capital's coach Bryan Murray answers questions during a postgame press conference.

Murray attributes his and the team's success over the last few years to "very good draft choices selected by our personnel director and our General Manager, David Poile. From the minute David and I came here, we adopted a defense-oriented philosophy for the organization. With the type of talent we had then, that was the best way for us to win the Stanley Cup."

Murray and Poile looked at the 26-36-18 team they inherited and realized they needed to overhaul their personnel with others who had already established a winning tradition. Poile engineered a trade with Montreal that brought in Rod Langway, Craig Laughlin, Doug Jarvis and Brian Engblom. Engblom was then traded for Larry Murphy, a first-round draft pick of the Los Angeles Kings in the 1980 draft.

"We ended up with four really established players, proven winners, in the 1981 training camp," recalls Murray. The crew that was brought in was tough and strong, and they dictated the revamped character of the team."

So Murray decided, "If we forecheck aggressively, we will always have a third man available to come back and help the defense. We stand in contrast to a number of teams in the league who are offensive minded. We don't give up a lot of easy chances against our goaltender." Given the team's turnaround with Murray and Poile at the helm, their decisions were wise ones indeed.

One of the most important jobs and most difficult challenges facing a coach is determining which individuals to pair together on three-man forward lines. "From being around the players and watching them practice every day, you get a feel for who works well together," explains Murray. "We put Mike Gartner and Bob Carpenter on the same line, because they both have great speed and are superb goal scorers. To those two, we added Gaetan Duchesne, an expert checker and passer."

What does a coach do before the game starts? Says Murray, "On every game day, we have a meeting in the morning, during which we go over the strategy we will use against our opponents. We tell the team how to forecheck, decide who should be in on the power plays, determine how to play in our own end, and describe their offensive and defensive schemes. Do they use an aggressive penalty-killing system or do they play a controlled or conservative system? How do they play in the neutral zone?"

What are the differences between coaching in the minors and in the big leagues? Murray explains, "At this level, there is more advanced scouting. You prepare harder for the other team and they do for you, than at the junior level. The personnel are better throughout the lineup, so you can do more as a coach. There is more of a star system in the juniors. Here, we have more people who can play the game at a higher level," so top players are less likely to act like prima donnas.

One surprise for Murray was that "I was always told that the dedication was not as great at the pro level. But players here are more committed than at the junior level, because these guys make their living from the sport. It is much harder motivating the bottom half of your squad in the juniors."

Not the least of the coach's challenges is handling the pressure from the fans, the media and from management to win. "I work hard and do as much as I can for the team," says Murray. "We all must be realistic. You get your guys to play to their highest level, and there's not a lot more you can do."

When he can't take the pressure anymore, he screams at referees "and that kind of lets off steam," admits the coach. These much maligned and underappreciated officials are the focus of our next chapter.

Chapter Six

Game Officials

The On-Ice Trio

Two linesmen and one referee, all fit and excellent skaters, compose the tandem that shares the ice with the players. All of these officials wear black trousers and official sweaters, and the referee is denoted by red (or orange) armbands on both of his arms.

Rarely do any of these dedicated arbiters receive kudos for jobs well done. Probably the highest form of accolade comes when players and coaches from both teams do not condemn the officials in postgame news conferences, or blame them for the misfortunes of their teams. As do officials in most professional sports, these men work in thankless jobs, and only rarely receive the pats on the back they often deserve.

Coaches and players constantly berate these men, and in particular the referee, who runs the show, for inconsistency in applying penalties equally to both teams within in a game. In fact, during the June meetings in Toronto for the 1985 draft, the NHL allocated $500,000 for a far-reaching study concerning the officiating of its games.

Another common criticism has been that different referees do not call their games the same way. But these men are only human and just as different coaches have opposite approaches to the game, so do referees see action with different sets of eyes and prejudices.

The linesman's task is much more mechanical and he

has less latitude in his decisions than does the referee. Linesmen work 80-85 games a year and earn from $30,000 to $55,000, exclusive of exhibition and playoff games. They call offsides and icing (described in Chapter Seven) and some minor infractions, as when too many men are on the ice or when an article is thrown on the playing surface (figure 23).

Figure 23.   Veteran linesman Gerard Gauthier warms up before the players make their appearance.

Occasionally, linesmen call major penalties that the referee does not see. These severe rules infractions, where injury often results, include spearing (stabbing an opponent with the point of the stick blade while the stick is being carried with one or both hands) and high sticking.

They may also stop play when pucks sail outside of the playing area and are interfered with by ineligible persons, when the goalpost has been dislodged from its normal position or when they observe that a goal has been scored and the referee did not. One more of the linesmen's duties is to drop the puck at all face-offs, except at the start of the game, at the beginning of each period and after a goal has been scored.

Unlike referees who rotate throughout the league, linesmen stay closer to home, and may do 50 percent of a home team's games. Referees supposedly work in each NHL city an equal number of times. They have no home games and long periods of travel can mean hardship to family men.

The most difficult part of his job, says Kerry Fraser, in his sixth year in the NHL as a referee, is "the travel and the time I'm away from my family. I have three little boys, and I miss important birthdays and holidays. Players complain about the travel, but they have 40 home games. We work 70, and they are all on the road," points out Fraser, who lives in Sarnia, Ontario (figure 24).

The referee takes total charge of the game and his decision in all disputes is final. This gutsy official, as important as the home-plate umpire in baseball, calls the majority of the penalties. His duty also is to inform the official scorer or the penalty timekeeper of all goals legally scored as well as to describe the infractions for which penalties have been imposed.

Aside from the excellent salary and the excitement of working in the big leagues, what motivates individuals to become referees? Fraser says he was practically born with skates on, played junior hockey and aspired to turn professional. "But," he recalls, "at the time when I got to draft age in the early 1970s, in the heyday of the Philadel-

Figure 24. Referees, like veteran Kerry Fraser, are denoted by their two red (orange) armbands.

phia Flyers, NHL teams were taking big players, and I was 5-foot-8, 150 pounds."

Fraser realized he didn't have the size or the ability to make it in the NHL but felt he did have a chance in the minors. Still, he saw no future in the lower echelons of the pros. A coach of the Detroit Red Wings suggested that he try referees' school.

"He thought I could keep pace with the players who were improving their abilities," says Fraser. "I didn't have the experience of officiating youth hockey. My training was as a player, which I feel allows me to have a little more compassion for their complaints."

So Fraser attended a one-week referee training school.

Canada has two sites for these courses, one in Ontario and one in the Maritimes. Following his graduation, Fraser spent three and a half seasons in the minors before joining the NHL.

Some may wonder whether it is legal for former players to become referees. "Certainly it is," responds Fraser. "As a matter of fact, we just had Paul Stewart, who played a few games with the Quebec Nordiques, go through a training program. As a kid growing up, you may have a favorite team or star, but once you put on a striped shirt, you become totally objective."

Fraser says the toughest call to make is the penalty shot. One of the rarest but most controversial of the referee's decisions, this call leads to thrilling moments for fans, who can observe the cat-and-mouse, one-on-one confrontation between shooter and goalie. In this situation, either the referee or the team designates a player who takes the puck from the center faceoff spot and then attempts to move in and score on the goaltender.

According to Fraser, this call has the most gray area for the referee. Many criteria must be satisfied before this ruling can be justified. "You may have a player in a full breakaway over the red line, and he is obviously fouled from behind. But for a penalty shot to be called, that player must have had full possession and control of the puck, and that is hard to determine if the puck is bouncing around," he says.

Another condition that must be satisfied is that the player with the puck must be taken down from behind. When the skater is hit from the side, this decision becomes clouded.

Penalty shots may also be awarded in situations where one player has deliberately tried to injure another. The referee may either call for a major penalty or a penalty shot. If the referee decides there was the intent to injure, even if a player is well protected and is shielded from harm, a penalty shot is warranted.

"It's the degree of violence," explains Fraser, "not specifically how bad the cut was. The old adage that blood has to be drawn for a penalty shot to be called is no longer applicable."

How does a referee put up with the taunts of the fans (figure 25) and the angry confrontations with upset players and coaches? "You have to be thick-skinned," answers Fraser. "Somebody is going to be upset whatever call you make. I'm confident in what I do, so I don't let that stuff bother me. If we do make a mistake, we have to be honest about it. If it's a case of a penalty being called and I didn't get a good look at it, or I overreacted, there's nothing I can do to change my decision.

Figure 25. Fans become emotionally involved and love to razz the opposition and officials.

"If a goal is called, I'll check with the goal judge, and the linesmen and make sure I've made the correct decision. I'll admit to players that I blew a call. It's not a case of making alibis, but admitting your error gets you more respect."

Fraser was the subject of some controversy during the 1985 playoffs. After a 2-1 Philadelphia win over Quebec in their series, Nordique coach Michel Bergeron ran a postgame videotape showing Flyer fouls allegedly overlooked by Fraser. Bergeron was fined $7,500 for his production. Referees do not have the luxury of reviewing slow-motion replays before making their calls, and such a display was not fair.

Although some veteran referees have garnered the respect of their peers, players and coaches, most of these officials are rarely praised. Far more frequently these arbiters on the ice are denigrated as being inconsistent.

Responds Fraser, "It's a bum rap. No two people think the same. We are not robots. We strive for consistency within ourselves and try to call the game the same way for both teams." Although we often expect them to be, referees are not infallible. Given the pressure on them and the speed with which they must make their decisions, they are vastly underappreciated.

More-damaging physical hazards are involved in the profession as well. "Even the most demure player in the league can explode," says Fraser. "When I was working a game in the American League, a player got a couple of penalties and was benched for not playing well. After he returned, I called another penalty on him. He threw his gloves down and came after me. I turned to face him and put both of my hands in front of me with palms open, in a defensive posture.

"I knew he would throw some punches at me and when he did, I grabbed his wrist and pulled him into me. By that time, players came over the boards and grabbed him. He ended up with a $10,000 fine."

Players' slap shots can also endanger officials. "Edmonton's Paul Coffey hit me with one and broke my ankle. It happened two minutes into the game. I knew it hurt but I never took off my skates between periods and finished the game on it. It blew up like a basketball," Fraser recalls.

To prevent such injuries, officials wear smaller versions of the players' **couperall,** a girdle-like football pad, which fits tightly around the waist and pads the kidneys, tailbone and thighs. They also use basketball-type kneepads, hard plastic shin pads, small elbow pads and some officials now wear helmets.

Overall, Fraser loves his work. "There is much more freedom than in most jobs. Each day is different. The fans and players can be screaming at me and it doesn't matter, as long as I know I've done the best I can. I just enjoy the game."

Minor Officials

Six minor officials occupy off-ice positions. **Goal judges** sit in glassed cages behind each goal. When a goal is claimed, the goal judge determines whether or not the puck passed between the goalposts and went completely over the goal line. A shot that moves halfway across the goal line does not count as a score.

To signal a goal, the goal judge (who does not switch goals during the game) flips a switch and turns on a red light above his cage. When the green light is activated, which signals the end of a period or a stoppage of play due to a penalty, no goal will count (figure 26).

Penalty timekeepers maintain records of all penalties meted out by officials. They note the names of guilty parties, the types of infractions, the lengths of the penalties and the times at which they were imposed. They make sure penalized players serve the allotted time in the penalty box and make certain penalties are correctly posted on the scoreboard.

Prior to game time, **official scorers** receive from the managers or coaches of both teams, a list of eligible

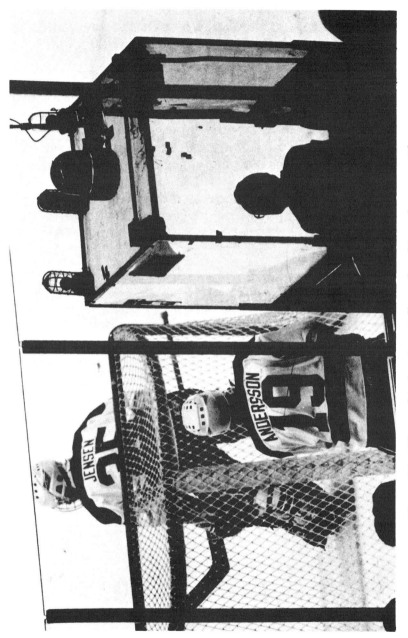

Figure 26.   The goal judge sits totally enclosed in a glass cage. The red signal on the left corner of the cage roof lights up on goal scores. The small green light in the middle marks a stop in play.

players, the starting lineups and the names of team captains. They list goals scored, the scorers and the players credited with assists. They sit high up in the stands and communicate via headsets with the public address announcers.

Game timekeepers record the time and signal the referee at the start and conclusion of each period. They give preliminary warnings to players in the locker rooms three minutes before the resumption of each period. Nineteen minutes into each of the three 20-minute periods, they notify the P.A. announcer that one minute remains.

Finally, **statisticians** record, on official league forms, all information relating to the performances of individual players of the two teams. They send their data sheets to the league president and to the visiting and home coaches or managers.

Chapter Seven

Icing, Offsides
and Additional Face-off Situations

Although hockey's object, scoring more goals than an opponent, is not complex, NHL hockey rules perplex newcomers to the sport and can confuse even veteran fans. Before digesting the most significant rules infractions, fans must first understand two technical violations which do not result in player penalty minutes: **icing** and **offsides.** These two terms can strike fear into the hearts of able broadcasters, for they are not easily explained. Nonetheless, let us proceed.

Icing

Icing occurs when a player of a team of equal or superior numerical strength to his opponent, shoots the puck from his team's half of the ice (divided by the red, checkered center line) across his opponent's goal line. If a rival, defending player other than the goaltender touches the puck before one of the shooter's teammates, the linesman signals icing by blowing his whistle. The puck then comes back to one of the large face-off circles (closest to the side of the rink from where the shot originated) in front of the goaltender of the team that iced the puck (figures 27 and 28).

When an attacking player who was onside when the puck was shot down the ice, touches it before an op-

goal line

blue line

center red line

Figure 27. This diagram shows the puck crossing the center red line, the blue line and then the goal line. In this situation, icing is called and the puck is then brought back to the opposite end of the ice for a face-off in the offending team's zone.

Figure 28. After blowing his whistle to stop the play and skating to the face-off spot, the linesman crosses his arms as shown, to indicate icing. The other linesman follows the puck over the red line and raises his arm to indicate to the pictured linesman to halt play.

ponent, no icing is called. If, in the opinion of a linesman, a defending player (aside from the goalie) can play the puck before it reaches his goal line but fails to do so, play also continues with no icing whistled (figure 29).

However, if the referee decides the defending side intentionally abstained from playing the puck promptly when in position to do so, he stops action and orders a face-off on the adjacent-corner face-off spot nearest the team at fault. Note that when linesmen make a mistake in signaling icing, the puck is faced on the center-ice face-off spot. Also important to remember is that when a team is playing short-handed because of a penalty, icing is permissable.

Sometimes icing benefits a team trying to break up an attack on its goal. When the defense is disorganized and under heavy pressure, icing is a better alternative than a goal score.

When skaters tire and a line change is needed but can't be performed smoothly, icing may prove a wise strategy. Finally, when a player is hurt or has broken or lost his stick, putting his team at a numerical disadvantage, icing is a good move.

Offsides

Offside violations come in two forms. When any member of the attacking team precedes his teammate carrying the puck over the defending team's blue line, an offside is called. The position of the player's skates, not that of his stick, constitutes the determining factor in this decision. If both skates are over the blue line before the puck, the player is offside. If he has only one skate over the blue line and one on it, straddling the involved line, he is onside.

When this rule is violated, play stops and the puck is then faced off in the neutral zone. Note that if a player controlling the puck crosses the blue line ahead of the puck, an offside is not called.

Figure 29. When this wash-out signal is used by the referee, a goal has been disallowed. When used by a linesman, this signal indicates no icing or no offside on the play.

Also, if the puck is cleanly intercepted by a member of the defending team at or near the blue line, and is then carried or passed by him into the neutral zone, the offside is overlooked and play continued. Finally, if a player legally carries or passes the puck back into his own defending zone while a player of the opposing team is in that zone, the offside is ignored and play continued.

The Two-Line Pass

The second offside variation occurs on passes. When a player passes the puck from his defending zone to a teammate beyond the center red line (thereby crossing the blue and red lines), the linesman signals an offside and orders a face-off at the originating point of the pass. The puck's position and not the player's skates (the criteria used on icing calls) determines from which zone the pass was made.

As stated in Rule 70 (a) of the 1984-85 official NHL rule book, "The puck may be passed by any player to a player of the same side within any one of the three zones into which the ice is divided, but may not be passed forward from a player in one zone to a player of the same side in another zone, except by a player on the defending team, who may make and take forward passes from their own defending zone to the center line without incurring an offside penalty. This "forward pass" from the defending zone must be completed by the pass receiver who is preceded by the puck across the center line, otherwise play shall be stopped and the face-off shall be at the point from which the pass was made."

Offensive teams never want to have their attacks stopped by an offside violation. But wingers on the team that does not have the puck sometimes try to push their men across the blue line, ahead of the puck, creating an offside situation and a halt in the action.

Additional Face-Off Situations

When either icing or offsides occur, play ceases and face-offs result. Many other situations exist where play stops and penalties are not called. If a player is held or interfered with by a spectator, the referee or linesman blows his whistle, stops play and faces off the puck at the spot where last played. If the team of the player interfered with is in possession of the puck, the play is completed before the whistle is blown.

When the puck sails outside of the rink or strikes any obstacles above the playing surface other than the boards or glass, it is faced off at the spot where it was shot or deflected. When a puck becomes lodged in the netting on the outside of either goal, or if it is intentionally frozen by two opposing players, the referee stops play and faces off the puck. If he decides the stoppage was caused by a player of the attacking team, the resulting face-off is held in the neutral zone.

A player is allowed to use an open hand to stop or bat a puck in the air. Play is not stopped unless, in the opinion of the referee, the player has deliberately directed the puck to a teammate. In that case, action is halted and the puck faced-off at the spot where the infraction occurred.

One other important rule to remember is that the puck has to be kept in motion at all times. A team in control of the puck in its own defensive zone, must advance the puck toward the opposing goal, unless prevented from doing so by opponents. For the first infraction of this rule, play is stopped and a face-off ensues at either end face-off spot adjacent to the goal of the team causing the stoppage. A second violation of this rule by a member of the same team in the same period leads to a minor penalty.

Since all of these situations result in face-offs, it would seem prudent to describe what happens on these calls in greater detail. The centermen taking the face-off stand almost nose to nose, with the blade of their sticks on the ice (figure 30). Visiting players place their sticks within the designated white area first. No other players are allowed to enter the face-off circle or to come within 15 feet of the players facing off the puck.

If a player facing off does not take his proper position immediately when directed to do so, the referee may order him replaced for that face-off by any teammate then on the ice. Many other situations can arise which result in face-offs, but these are the principal ones. Penalties, where one or more players leave the ice and serve varying amounts of time in the penalty box, depending on the severity of the infraction, will be the subject of our next chapter.

Figure 30. On face-offs, centermen focus on the linesman's hand rather than on the spot on the ice where the puck will land.

Chapter Eight

Penalties

Penalties fall into six distinct categories, which include the following divisions: minor penalties, bench minor penalties, major penalties, misconduct penalties, match penalties and penalty shots. To list every form of infraction and their resulting consequences would be too complex for the intent of this book. Therefore, only the most common and significant representatives of these subgroups have been selected.

Referees, unless their views are obstructed, call all of these offenses. The decision whether to impose a minor penalty or one of the more severe alternatives is, in many cases, up to their discretion. The following synopses describe the six types of rules infractions and list examples from each category.

A.   On **minor** penalties, any player other than the goaltender can be sent off the ice and into the penalty box for two minutes, during which time no substitute is permitted. The following eight violations are typical:

1. Tripping

Any player who intentionally uses his stick, knee, foot, arm, hand or elbow to cause his opponent to trip or fall receives a minor (figure 31).

2. Holding

A two-minute penalty results when a player grabs or holds an opponent with his hands or stick for any length of time, thereby knocking him off stride (figures 32 and 33).

3. Broken Stick

A forward or defenseman must immediately drop his broken stick or be liable for a two-minute minor penalty. However, a goaltender may continue to play with a broken stick, with no penalty called.

4. Delay of Game

Any skater who intentionally delays the game by using his stick to shoot or bat the puck outside of the playing area is guilty of this infraction.

5. Falling on the Puck

No defending player aside from the goaltender can fall on or use his hands to gather in a puck.

6. Roughing

Players, who after having been punched, retaliate with a blow of their own, can be charged with a minor. The third man in on a fight is automatically ejected from the game. Referees are given wide latitude in deciding on the severity of their sanction for this offense (figure 34).

Figure 32. Holding

Figure 31. The following signals are given by the referee to the penalty timekeeper to indicate an infraction. The official pictured is Brad Kent, a past president and 10-year member of the Southeastern Hockey Officials Association (SHOA). Kent has worked many junior, amateur and collegiate games. Here he demonstrates the tripping call.

Figure 33.   Here is a clear example of a holding violation.

83

7. Handling Pucks with Hands

Aside from the goaltender (who may hold the puck for three seconds), no skater can close his hand on the puck. It is permitted to stop or bat a puck in the air, as long as the puck has not been deliberately directed to a teammate. In that case, action stops and the puck is faced off where the offense occurred.

8. Interference

One may not impede an opponent not in possession of the puck, deliberately knock the stick out of an opponent's hand or prevent a player from regaining possession of the stick (figure 35).

B. **Bench minors,** which occur on or in the immediate vicinity of the player's bench but off the playing surface, involve the removal of one player of the offending team, for two minutes. Any player aside from the goaltender can be designated to serve the penalty, by the manager or coach of the penalized team.

This rule applies to any player who does not proceed directly to the penalty box, when directed to do so by the referee. In addition, bench minors are called when there are too many men on the ice and can be slapped on team officials in the vicinity of the team bench, who throw objects on the ice during the game.

C. For the first **major penalty** imposed, the offender, unless it is the goaltender, leaves the ice for five minutes. An automatic $50 fine accompanies major penalties for any foul causing injury to the face or head of an opponent through use of a stick. When a player receives his third major in a game, he is banished from the ice for the evening. A substitute is allowed after five minutes have elapsed. After this third offense, the guilty player is automatically slapped with a $100 fine.

The referee must decide whether or not the infraction involved an intent to injure, in determining whether an infraction warranted a major or minor penalty. **Butt-ending** means hitting a competitor with the butt end of the stick, dangerous in its potential impact on the face and eyes. **Spearing,** stabbing an opponent with the point of the stick blade while the stick is being carried with one or both hands, is viewed as a deliberate attempt to injure. Both violations are punished with major penalties.

    D. **Misconduct penalties** to all skaters except the goaltender require the offending party or parties to leave the game for 10 minutes (figure 36). Substitutes may immediately replace the player or players serving the penalty, which leads to an automatic $50 fine. The player must remain in the penalty box after the 10 minutes have elapsed, until the next stop in action.

These penalties are justified when, for example, players unleash obscene, profane or abusive language. They are also called for when any person intentionally knocks or shoots the puck out of the reach of an official trying to retrieve it or when players, in anger, intentionally smash the boards with their sticks.

In the last couple of years, more two-minute unsportsmanlike-conduct penalities have been called for the aforementioned infractions. Two-minute short-handed situations can prove much more costly than $50 fines. **Game misconduct penalties** result in a player's suspension for the rest of the game, a fine of $100 and a report filed with the league president. The president may impose further penalties if he so chooses. A substitute may immediately replace the removed player. This penalty is enforced on any player or goalkeeper who is the first to intervene in a fight then in progress, on any player who continues fighting after being ordered to stop by the referee and on any player who deliberately hits an

Figure 34.   Roughing

Figure 35.   Interference

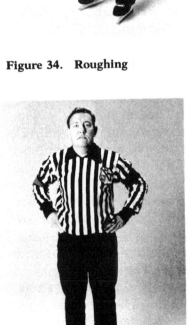

Figure 36.   Misconduct Penalty

official (resulting in a 20-game suspension).

Referees may impose gross misconduct penalties on any player, manager, coach or trainer guilty of such behavior. Those individuals are given the same sanctions as those receiving game misconduct penalties.

During the regular season, any player who gets three game misconduct penalties is suspended for the next league game. In playoff games, any player who receives two such penalties is suspended for the next playoff game of his team.

E. **Match penalties** for intentionally trying to injure an opponent (e.g., head butting or kicking) involve the dismissal of a player for the rest of the game. A substitute is permitted after 10 minutes, when the guilty player has deliberately injured an opponent, and after five minutes if he failed in his attempt to harm his competitor.

F. **Penalty shots** may be awarded under the following conditions: (a) when players deliberately displace a goal-post during a breakaway, (b) when a player in control of the puck in the opponent's side of the center red line, having no other opponent to pass than the goalkeeper, is interfered with by a stick or any other object (inter-ference), (c) when a player illegally enters the game, (d) when any member of the defending team throws a stick or any other object at the puck in the defending zone, (e) for fouling from behind, (f) for deliberate illegal substitu-tion with insufficient playing time left and (g) for falling on or (h) picking up the puck in the crease.

The name of the player selected by the referee or desig-nated by the team from among the players on the ice (depending on the infraction) is then announced over the P.A. system. The puck is placed on the center face-off spot and the player taking the shot then moves in on the goaltender. Once the puck crosses the attacking blue line, it must be kept in motion towards the opponent's goal line. Once the puck is shot, the play is considered complete.

Many infractions can result in either major or minor penalties, depending on the referee's determination of their degree of malice. The nine violations that follow are among the most common:

1. Fighting

Fighting generally occurs when players drop their gloves and engage in fist fights. A major penalty is usually assessed to the participants.

2. High Sticks

Players may not carry their sticks above shoulder height when moving in on a direct confrontation with an opponent. Neither can they bring their stick up on a rival, thereby hitting him above the shoulders. Goals scored from sticks held in this manner are disallowed. When injury to the face or head results from such an infraction, the referee must impose a major penalty on the offending player (figure 37).

3. Hooking

Hooking involves using the stick or stick blade to hold back an opponent, usually by snaring his waist, arm or neck (figures 38 and 39). Again, when injury results, a major is mandatory. When a player checks another in such a way that there is only stick-to-stick contact, neither hooking nor holding should be called.

4. Slashing

Slashing occurs when one player uses his stick to strike another player in his leg, pants or hands, generally in

Figure 37.   High Sticks

Figure 38.   Hooking

89

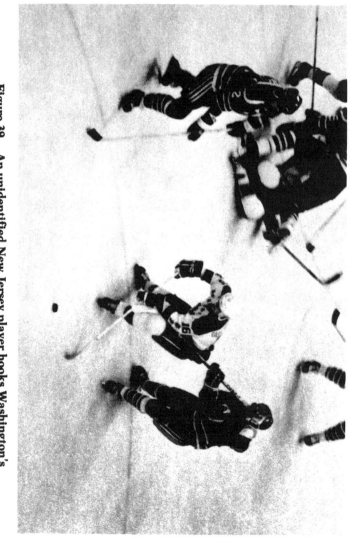

Figure 39. An unidentified New Jersey player hooks Washington's Bengt Gustafsson, one of the many Europeans playing in the NHL today. Gustafsson was raised in Karlskoga, Sweden.

anger or in retaliation (figure 40). When injury or the intent to cause harm are detected, majors are warranted. Referees should invoke this penalty both when a player swings his stick at a rival (whether in or out of range) and does not actually strike him or if a player, pretending to play the puck, takes a wild swing, with the object of intimidating an opponent.

5. Charging

A minor or major penalty should be called if a player runs (using two or more steps or strides), jumps or charges into an opponent (figure 41). This rule is also applied to offending players who ram a goalkeeper who is within his goal crease. A goalie is not fair game when he moves outside of this area. Unnecessary contact justifies a penalty for interference or charging.

6. Cross-Checking

A variation of high sticking, cross-checking means holding the stick at each end, parallel to the ice and, like a warrior in the Middle Ages, using it to ram an opponent across the chest, back of the neck or back (figure 42).

7. Spearing

Stabbing an opponent with the point of the stick blade constitutes spearing. A jabbing motion with hands together, thrust in front of the chest, indicates this violation (figure 43).

8. Elbowing and Kneeing

As the name of this penalty implies, a minor or major is imposed when a player uses his elbow or knee in such a manner as to foul an opponent.

Figure 40.   Slashing

Figure 41.   To signal charging, referees rotate clenched fists around on another, in front of their chests.

Figure 42.   Cross-Checking

Figure 43.   Spearing

Figure 44. Elbowing

Figure 45. Boarding

Figure 46. Delayed Penalty

93

9. Boarding

Depending on the degree of violence of the impact, a minor or major penalty is imposed on any player who illegally checks or elbows an opponent into the boards (figure 45).

What happens once a penalty is detected? That depends on which team has control of the puck when the penalty is signaled. If team A is carrying the puck and team B commits an infraction, the referee will delay the penalty and not blow his whistle until A loses possession.

Referees signal penalties by holding one arm up in the air, and pointing with the other at the penalized player. Often, on delayed penalties (figure 46), A's goaltender will leave the ice, replaced by an extra forward, until B touches the puck. If the team in control of the puck commits the penalty, action is halted immediately.

Before leaving this subject area, one more term must be defined. Frequently, after fights, two players are penalized and head for the penalty box to serve their time simultaneously. On majors over five minutes, such penalties are called **coincidental.**

Chapter Nine

Shots and Passes of the Game

Of the variety of shots skilled hockey players must master, the most common are the **slap shot** (perfected by Bun Cook in the 1920s) and the **wrist shot.** Youngsters learn the slap shot before any other. This full-blast, crowd-pleasing stroke which can send pucks at speeds between 90 and 120 miles per hour, starts with a big backswing. The stick is then propelled down at the puck (which should be lined up with the front skate), hits directly behind it and the swing concludes with a complete follow through.

Best results are achieved by hitting the ice slightly behind the puck, right in the middle of the stick blade. Contact off the tip or the heel of the stick leads to errant shots. Righthanders usually place their right hand at the top of the stick (**left shots**) and lefthanders reverse this procedure (**right shots**). The lower hand position varies according to the type of shot attempted and on the situation.

For example, when players **stickhandle** (moving the puck from backhand to forehand and back again), hands are held close to one another, providing the player with the maximum amount of feel necessary to deftly maneuver the puck. When passing, players slide the bottom hand a bit lower on the stick, which allows them to generate a bit more power than when stickhandling. When players decide to shoot, they move the lower hand down the stick's handle as far as possible, leading to increased force behind the shot.

On **slap shots,** the follow through dictates the direction the puck will take. A high finish with the stick blade open sends the puck high, while a lower one with a closed face lowers the puck's trajectory and keeps it down on the ice. The curvature in the stick also helps determine where the puck will go and how it will react once it takes off. The blade curve can make the puck dive, rise up or knuckle like a baseball pitch, making the goaltender's job that much more difficult.

Most goals in the NHL today, especially those scored from beyond 40 feet, come off slap shots, not true 20 years ago. In those days, the most commonly used shot was the more accurate, forehand **wrist shot,** which has no backswing and is done from within 35 feet of the net.

On wrist shots, which have little or no wind up, hands are held much closer together than on a slap shot. The bottom wrist on the stick directs and helps to elevate the puck. The hand above grips securely and holds the top of the stick to assist in control. To excel at this shot requires superior hand, forearm and wrist strength, which accounts for those areas being overdeveloped in many of of the great shooters.

The **snap shot** combines the slap and wrist shots. Here the stick is brought back a foot or two and then snapped through like a wrist shot. The snap shot has more accuracy than the faster slap shot and is nearly as accurate as the wrist shot.

Because hockey stick blades are now curved, the **backhand shot** (figure 47) is seldom used. Shooting backhanded could be compared with using the back of a boomerang. Much more common today is the **deflected shot.**

Although deflections look like they always come by accident, that is not always the case. Many teams become adept at their use through drills in practice. According to the plan, a defenseman shoots the puck from the point, trying to keep his shot low. Forwards position themselves about 15 feet in front of the net and attempt to deflect the puck. Just the slightest touch can change the

Figure 47.   Mike Gartner prepares to take a backhand shot against New Jersey.   Goaltender Ron Low has moved out to cut down the angle.

puck's direction four to six feet. The goaltender, already committed in the direction of the slap shot, has no way to recover.

No shot proves ideal for all players. The best shot alternative is determined by the distance of the puck from the goal, by how much time is available to get the shot off, and by the angle that the puck must take to find its way into the net. Attacking players should make every effort to both shield the goaltender's vision and to select the most sensible of the shot options, not necessarily the most flashy.

Three Passes

Before leaving this topic, it seems logical to mention the several types of passes common in hockey. Ideally, the pass, which leads the receiver, should be made with the receiver in full skating stride. The puck should arrive in a flat position, easy for the receiver to handle. Players must anticipate their linemate's moves, keep their heads up and accurately hit their targets.

On the most commonly used **forehand pass,** the stick moves ahead maintaining a low trajectory to the ice. On **drop passes,** the passer leaves the puck deadened by stickhandling and drops off the puck for a trailing teammate. **Flip passes** are recommended when a defensive player stands between the passer and the receiver. Instead of risking a forehand pass that could be easily picked off, the passer flips the puck up off the toe of his stick, sending the puck up and past the defender. This maneuver also works when it is necessary to clear the puck against the boards into center ice.

The NHL stars of today are masters of all these shots and passes. Nonetheless, although the high goal scorers receive the lion's share of the publicity, hockey is a team sport. No one player can carry a team by himself. Even Gretzky owes much of his success to his splendid support crew.

It is the head coach's job to establish effective offensive and defensive systems of play. Those topics seem the next logical areas to explore.

Chapter Ten

Offensive and Defensive Strategies

Headmanning the Puck

Successful offenses continuously headman the puck, until it reaches the opposition blue line, where plays may be set up. **Headmanning** means to keep the puck moving forward to the lead skater in the attack. A team only gets in trouble when the puck is brought back into its own end.

Offensive teams that control their opponent's blue lines force defenses to back up on their goaltenders. Stan Mikita, a past star of the Chicago Black Hawks, was an expert on the **center rush.** During this play, he would race down the ice as fast he could. Suddenly he would slam on the brakes as soon as he moved a couple of steps inside the defender's blue line.

If the two rival defensemen did not **stand up** at the blue line to meet him, Mikita would gain control of the area just inside the blue line. From that position he would either shoot or wait until one of his wingers broke toward the net. If the defensemen did come out to check him, Mikita would act like a quarterback, and wait for his wingers to break for the net. As soon as they made their move, he would headman the puck and get them in a position to shoot.

To counteract this offensive ploy, defensemen must stand up at the blue line. Assuming their wingers pick up their attacking counterparts, the defensemen move up on the center and try to halt his rush, at the blue line.

Breakouts and Breakaways

Teams generally utilize two methods of getting the puck out of their own defensive zone: the **controlled breakout,** and if they are lucky, the **breakaway.** Breakouts occur after an attacker misses his shot on goal. A rival defenseman retrieves the puck behind his own net and stops. The center then generally circles back and either picks up the puck from his defenseman and starts moving it up the ice or he fakes that move and takes off toward the other end. In that case, the defenseman tries to hit his center with a pass.

If the center does not come back into the defensive zone, the defenseman may wait for his wingers to set up on the hash marks of the face-off circle near the boards. He then moves out on one side of the net and delivers a crisp pass to one of his wings.

Sometimes also, one defenseman under pressure may pass to his fellow defenseman, who passes the puck to the center, near the middle of the ice, about 25 feet from the net. The center then tries to move the puck to his wing, who continues the breakout. Which one of the breakouts is employed varies according to the forechecking or defensive scheme used by the other team.

On breakaways, a defensive error has been made allowing an attacker to move in by himself on the opponent's goaltender. As on a penalty shot, the resulting play is one of the most exciting in all of hockey, leading to either a goal score or a spectacular save by the goaltender.

When the attacker approaches the goalie head-on, he should aim for either corner of the net, from about 15 feet out. From the wing, he can either shoot or fake the shot and try to slip the puck by the goaltender.

Breakaways can occur when a defenseman falls down, leaving his man free to move in on the goal unimpeded. Another typical breakaway situation arises when a defenseman has his slap shot blocked by a forward at the blue line, providing the interceptor with a clear pathway down the ice.

Power Plays

Power plays account for about 25% of a team's goals during the season. After penalties, when one team has a one- or two-man advantage over its opponents, power plays result. The strategy during these situations is to continuously move the puck closer to the net, until one player breaks free and becomes isolated near the goal. Hopefully, a teammate will spot the open man and hit him with a pass. The free skater should then waste little time getting off his shot and needs to make it count.

Nowadays, NHL clubs are so specialized that they seek out those adept at scoring in these situations. Many hours in practice are devoted to proper execution of the power play.

As Stan and Shirley Fischler point out in their well-researched *Everybody's Hockey Book,* "The power play actually begins the second the penalty takes place, because as soon as the referee raises his hand to indicate an infraction, the team about to have the player advantage should try to pull their goalie and put the extra skater on the ice. As long as the offending team does not touch the puck, the referee cannot whistle the end of play. Thus, the first maneuver in a power play situation is to keep possession of the puck and get the extra skater on the ice—even if it means skating all the way back into their own defensive zone to set the play up." [1]

Recall that on power plays, **penalty killers** may knock the puck into the attacker's end of the ice without icing being called. To avoid those quick slaps which burn off the clock, power plays generally start behind the attackers' net. Typically, the center or a defenseman initates the up-ice procedure. Wings stay close to the puck carrier, to avoid long passes which could be easily picked off.

When defenders are one man short, they set up a

---

1. *Everybody's Hockey Book,* Stan and Shirley Fischler, Charles Scribner's Sons, New York, 1983, p. 286.

square-shaped, **box zone defense.** Two forwards stay out at opposite ends, just inside the blue line. Defensemen set up about five feet in front of their net and also play a zone, moving toward the side the puck is on.

Attackers have many methods of penetrating and opening up a hole in the box. An offensive player may skate to its center, forcing one defender to abandon his position. Another choice is to flood one side of the box by setting up three attackers on one end. This action forces the two corner players on one side of the box to come out and commit themselves.

Usually, on power plays, one or two skaters try to jam up the area in front of the net and thereby screen the goaltender's vision. When such a traffic pile-up is created, forwards, inserted at the point in these situations because of their scoring abilities, will wind up and take a slap shot.

They try to keep these shots down for two reasons. Low shots are both easier to deflect and are also less dangerous than high-flying pucks. Wings playing close in don't have the padding of a goaltender. A puck heading for their eyes or bodies at 90 miles an hour could do serious damage.

Defenders forming the four corners of the box need to stay disciplined and remain in their zone coverage unless forced out. Killing penalties is tiring work. As a result, teams usually have two or three sets of penalty killers, who take the ice for at least 45 seconds at a time.

When teams run two men short after a penalty, they set up in a three-cornered, **triangle defense** (figure 48). The moving point of the triangle starts with one man up-ice in the slot area, about 40 feet from the net. His job is to cover both points, interfere with and perhaps intercept the quick passes between the offensive point men and to avoid being faked out.

Of course, one man cannot last very long skating between the two point positions. Let's look at an example of an attack on a triangle defense. Suppose the puck is passed to the right side. The point man at the top of the

48. The defensive team playing a triangle defense as they defend against a 4-on-3 power play.

triangle will move to that side to cover. When the puck is then shifted to the left side, the left defenseman who was deep at the base of the triangle will go out to help. The point of the triangle then shifts toward the goal.

The Three-on-Two Rush

In this common situation, three offensive players, usually forwards, race down the ice. This trio is guarded by two defenders, not counting the goaltender. Actually, this rush constitutes a three-on-three break, but in hockey terminology, it is a three-on-two. Theoretically, one man should always be open. The center, who should then be carrying the puck, must find a way to get the puck to his free linemate.

Although the center has a number of options, one favorite play is to have two of the forwards force the play up against the defensemen. Just before the defensemen come out to meet these two, the attacker with the puck drops it back to the open **"trailer."** He then moves in on the net, with his two linemates running interference for him.

Defenders must try to stand up against the three charging attackers. Defensemen cannot back up too far into their zone without risking putting their goaltender in a position he can not handle. Therefore, defenders must force the man with the puck away from the center, while staying in front of the puck carrier.

The Two-on-One Break

In this situation, the best strategy for the offensive player is to force the solitary defender to commit himself. As soon as he accomplishes that task, he can easily pass the puck to his unguarded teammate, who is free to move in on the goalie unimpeded. If the defenseman holds his position and does not go for a fake, the attacker should take the shot before losing his angle on the goal.

The goaltender's job in the two-on-one is to play the man with the puck. The defenseman, who stays in the middle of the ice, tries to prevent the man without the puck from getting it and attempts to force the puck carrier to shoot off target. If a pass is made, he should be in position to steal it, or to at least disrupt the receiver's timing.

One important decision for a coach to make, as Bryan Murray pointed out earlier in the book, is how to position the team's forward line. He must decide whether his squad should focus on piling up the points or on doing whatever possible to prevent opponents from scoring.

Of course, ideally, teams aim to accomplish both of these goals. In fact, most rosters are not so well balanced and talent laden that they can meet both obligations. The scales must therefore be tipped in either an offense- or defense-oriented direction.

The Fischlers addressed this quandary. They write,

"Some general rules apply to attacking play in the offensive zone. A team in possession of the puck must always think offensively, but it is essential at the same time to keep one player from the forward line in a position to back-check and aid the defense if the puck should be lost. Simultaneously it is to a team's advantage to keep a forward planted in front of the net, thereby occupying one whole defender and putting a man in position for a quick shot."[2]

Just as significant as creating a team's offensive character, is selecting a defensive forechecking scheme for the skaters to follow. That topic, different types of legal checks and the strategy behind line changes are described next.

2. Ibid, p. 280

Chapter Eleven

Checking and Line Changes

Forechecking

Just as headmanning the puck constitutes the essence of offense, checking forms the body and soul of defense in hockey. Something like a pressing system in basketball, **forechecking** can be defined as the defensive scheme used on opponents working on moving the puck out of its end of the ice.

One object of forechecking is to tie up opponents deep in their own zone, preventing them from initiating an attack from behind their own blue line. The second goal of forechecking is to steal back the puck, allowing the offense to resume its charge in the opponent's half of the rink.

Teams may utilize one of several basic forechecking systems, all of which require that at least three men play back. Frequently, the center starts the forechecking by moving in at an angle and halting the forward movement of the puck carrier.

If that man skates to his right, the center's left-wing linemate moves in to double team. If the puck carrier takes the other route, it is the right wing's job to stop his flow. All three forwards cannot get involved at once without facing the risk of opponents shaking off the forechecking and starting a break up the ice.

An essential rule followed by those forechecking is to play the man and not the puck, thereby preventing the wings from breaking out. In a man-to-man forechecking scheme, wingers match up against opposing wingers. The center covers his counterpart. One defenseman plays the puck carrier and the other defenseman comes in to pick up the loose puck.

Body Checking

Body checking, as its name implies, means taking a man out of the play or preventing him from getting control of the puck by legally using the body or the stick. Players must not run more than two steps before doling out their check and cannot use unnecessary force to slam an opponent into the boards. Failure to observe these restrictions can result in a player being slapped with a charging violation.

Body checks, which require split-second timing, must be carefully executed to avoid a breakaway situation. They are also not the best moves for outnumbered checkers.

But when the puck carrier is either preoccupied with controlling a pass or is skating along with his head down, oblivious to the oncoming defender, a crushing body check can be both intimidating and effective. Expert body checkers ram their shoulders into their opponents' chests, separating them from the puck as well as sometimes from their senses.

The rather spectacular **hip check,** which can result in a victim flying head over heels, is another body-check variation in the defenseman's bag of tricks. This defensive weapon works well against puck carriers skating along the boards.

The hip checker skates backward on an angle, pretending to give his opponent enough room to move around him. When the skaters reach a position parallel to one another, the checker uses his hip to take out his opponent's legs.

The **poke check** is a good tool for any defender working

one-on-one. It is particularly effective for forechecking forwards pressuring puck carriers, for backskating defensemen and for penalty killers. Facing his attacking rival, the defender, making sure not to hold or grab, uses his stick to take a one-handed poke at the puck.

Many other check variations are available to the complete hockey player. Those mentioned are only the most common.

Line Changes

Because they happen so quickly and with such regularity, **line changes** can confuse new fans to the ice-hockey world. When do they occur? How long do players stay on the ice? What strategy is involved? Do all five players leave the ice together? How do the players know when to leave the ice? These are all questions novice hockey fans would like to have answered.

The first chance a home coach has to impact on a game is when he receives the visiting team's opening line, prior to game time. His job, then, is to put out a line of his own which will counteract the strengths and take advantage of the weaknesses of the on-ice group selected by the rival coach. When the opponent's line includes their best offensive player, the home coach quite often will insert his top-flight defensive unit to work against him.

Three-man forward lines and two-man defensive pairs remain on the ice for 45 to 90 seconds. The defensive duos usually last a bit longer than the faster-skating forwards. The idea is that when one of the forwards leaves the ice, the two remaining forwards should follow suit, to keep the units together (figures 49 and 50).

As soon as the left winger comes toward the bench, within about 15 feet, that signals the next forward line (one of four the team keeps) to get up and take the ice. Everyone tires at different times, but the centerman and right wing linemates of the left wing know they must exit as well, even if they are not fatigued. Defensemen—

49. Players change lines on the fly, while one defenseman lines up on an oncoming forward.

Figure 50. After action stops, players change lines at a more relaxed tempo.

teams usually include three tandems—also conform to the 15-foot rule.

A line change should never be attempted by a team when the puck is in their end of the ice. Forwards should only change when the play is in the offensive zone. If a switch is made when the action takes place in the defensive zone, the opponents are furnished with a free, momentary power play. Foolhearty though that action seems, it is a fairly commonplace practice of an undisciplined hockey player.

As championships often rest on the play of quarterbacks in football, pitchers in baseball and centers in basketball, goaltenders carry that burden on the hockey rink. When a mistake is made by a teammate, they must prevent that error from leading to a score. They have to rally their club when it needs a lift, act as the backbone to the defense, stand up grimfaced to the criticism of the fans and media and rise to the occasion during the playoffs.

Without a great goaltender in the net, teams stand little chance of taking the Stanley Cup. This solitary man who has the weight of the team on his shoulders is so crucial that the next chapter has been devoted to his role.

Chapter Twelve

Goaltending

Without question, the goaltender forms the hub of the hockey team, both figuratively and literally. All of the action centers around his entrenchment on the rink. Players skate around him and at him at dizzying speeds. Rock-hard pucks are blasted at this last bastion of defense, who must use lightning-fast reflexes, his vision, equipment and his body to prevent the projectiles from crossing the goal line.

He must have intelligence enough to outwit attackers, skate backwards as well as a defenseman and possess great flexibility. This solitary man in a team sport has to show courage in the face of desperate odds and must never back down from an intimidating opponent (figure 51). His job is to lead his club through his clutch play. He must be in good condition as well, for he is the only man (aside from the officials) to remain on the ice, without respite, for the game's duration.

Naturally, some goaltenders play more pivotal roles on certain teams than on others. For example, the great Ken Dryden was not as important to the offensively explosive, talent-laden Montreal Canadiens as was Bernie Parent to the Philadelphia Flyers. One reason Dryden retired was that he felt nothing else could be accomplished playing for a team like Montreal.

One quality that separates a good goaltender from a great one is concentration. Every goalie who reaches the big leagues has superior speed and reflexes. He could not

Figure 51. **Washington's Greg Adams attempts to clear out the front of his net as Vancouver's Patrick Sundstrom fights for position. Goaltender Pat Riggin did not back down, but as a consequence, was buried under the pile.** Photo by J. Henson Photographics.

have gotten that far without those assets. But concentration, as in individual sports like golf and tennis, delineates those at the higher echelons of the sport from the rest of the pack (figure 52).

Goaltenders face many distractions, both from the crowd just behind them and from the bodies flying around in front of the net. They must keep their minds totally on the job at hand and forget about any goals allowed earlier. They must never grow overconfident in a sport where the tide can turn in a matter of seconds.

A popular misconception about goaltenders is that they need not excel at skating. It is true that goaltenders

Figure 52.   Goalies like the Capital's Al Jensen act as the last line of defense. Jensen's wide-open eyes mark his concentration on stopping the fast-moving puck in front of him.   Photo by Gary Fine.

do not have to have the ability to race down the length of the ice. But they must be very quick on their feet and cannot spend much time on their backs or rumps. After falling, goaltenders must jump up in a hurry, a skill only accomplished through well-honed skating skills and by those with strong upper bodies and legs.

Goaltenders must be fairly strong to remain mobile with their heavy equipment. Full gear may weigh close to 40 pounds and by the third period, with absorbed perspiration and moisture from the ice, may rise five to 10 pounds above that level. It is not uncommon for a goaltender to lose 10 pounds during the course of the game.

Although they appear to have the most dangerous position on the ice, goaltenders are very well protected from injury. The only area vulnerable to a stick or puck is the neck. In fact, most current NHL goaltenders protect that area as well. Cage masks, similar to those worn by catchers in baseball, offer improved protection compared with the old-fashioned, solid, molded-fiberglass models. Those masks fitted so securely on the skin, that pucks striking around the openings caused some severe abrasions.

Until the early 1960s, goaltenders could not wear face protectors without being ridiculed as having lost their nerve. Jacques Plante, of the Montreal Canadiens, forever altered that silly notion one night in Madison Square Garden in a game against the New York Rangers. Ranger player Andy Bathgate hit Plante with a shot in the nose. In those days, teams dressed only one goaltender.

Plante went into the dressing room and had his wound stiched up. To the crowd's disbelief, he returned to the ice donning a mask, previously worn on occasion in practices but never in a game. Although not wearing a mask seems reckless to us now, in those times sticks were not curved and pucks did not travel at such high speeds.

Goaltenders focus on cutting down the shooter's angle at the open net. The goaltender uses the outside corners of the rectangular goal crease to line himself up in such a way as to show as little open net as possible to a shooter coming in on a wing.

Nets are six-feet wide and four-feet high. If the goaltender stays in the net, he provides a four-foot window through which players can shoot. By moving out, he may cut down on, and if done properly, eliminate that glimpse of uncovered net.

Bernie Parent was so adept at cutting angles, that some aficionados were prompted to comment that he could have played the game sitting in a rocking chair. He cut the angles so perfectly that very little movement was necessary on his part. Naturally, larger goaltenders have an easier time cutting angles, making it even more crucial for smaller goalies to master this skill.

How do goalies decide whether to use a glove, skate or stick to make a save? If the puck is off the ice, they should use their gloves as much as possible, to help cut down on the chance of giving up a goal on a rebound. Drives skimming along the ice surface are better stopped with sticks and skates.

Goaltenders who come out of the net to cut angles, use their pads or chest to stop the puck. Goaltenders who play for subpar teams do not have the chance to venture far out of their net. To do so, they must be sure that the defensemen or wings will not lose men breaking toward the net.

Goaltenders must communicate with their defensemen and forwards. A goalie can go out and look great cutting down an angle and forcing an individual to pass off the puck. If that man hits a winger open through a defensive lapse, the goalie will look like a fool as his opponent shoots into an open net.

Good communication can mean the difference between a save and disaster. Remember, when a puck comes down toward his end, the goaltender has a good view of the play as it develops. His defensemen have their backs to the play and don't know what's happening behind them. So the goaltender yells out instructions to his teammates like, "He's right on you. Move behind the net." He provides defensemen with eyes in the backs of their heads.

Sometimes the goaltender has to act like a sixth forward, able to pass the puck ahead to create plays. For example, errant long-distance shots taken from center ice may travel around the boards. Unalert goaltenders who do not stop the puck from making a complete circle, allow the offensive team to pick up the loosepuck deep in their opponent's defensive zone.

To prevent this situation, goaltenders try to race behind the net and hold the puck for one of their defensemen. Meanwhile, a rival winger has wasted a lot of energy skating after a puck that will never reach him.

If this play is executed properly, the goaltender can pass the puck forward, thereby trapping two players in the defensive zone. Former New York Ranger and Detroit Red Wing goalie Eddie Giacomin refined this skill to an art and may have been the best passer at his position in NHL history.

Just as baseball pitchers keep an imaginary and sometimes real book on opposition batters, so do goalies hold mental pictures of a rival player's tendencies in particular situations. Some individuals will tip off that they are about to shoot by putting their heads down. Others like to stick handle around the goalie. Some players shoot best from a certain distance or angle from the net. Another aspect of goaltending, then, is outguessing an opponent and anticipating his moves.

Strategically, goaltenders basically play a zone defense. Whatever side of the rink the puck goes to, they move toward, as do players in a zone defense in basketball. They may cheat a little if they anticipate a pass, but the next time the attacker faces the same situation, he will fake the pass and take the shot as soon as the goalie moves out of his zone.

A cardinal sin in hockey is to allow a goal from the "short side," the end of the net closest to the shooter. If the goalie and his defenseman are doing their jobs, short-side goals should never occur.

Goalies use a variety of moves and styles of play. Hall-of- Fame-goalie Glen Hall, of the Chicago Black Hawks and the St. Louis Blues, was an advocate of the **"butterfly"** move, with knees together, legs spread out and back bent backwards. The advantage of this posture is that the leg spread covers more area close to the ice. On the other hand, the upper part of the net may be more open than if another move was used (figure 53).

The **"standup"** goaltender represents another style alternative, especially suitable for taller players. Here the goalie stays up on his skates and only goes down when trying to smother a puck. Just the opposite of the butterfly style, the standup movement works better on high shots than on low ones.

Some goalies are known as intimidators and one has come to be known as hockey's No. 1 villain. The New York Islander's Billy Smith led his team to four straight Stanley Cups, between 1980 and 1983. The goalie with the most playoff wins (88) had helped his team to 19 consecutive playoff victories, until that streak was stopped by Edmonton in 1984.

During that series, Smith caught a lot of flak for using his stick to trip Gretzky, towards the end of the second game. Gretzky criticized the play as dirty, prompting Smith to respond, "Gretzky had a chance to clear me and he didn't. That bothered me. I lost some respect for him because of it."

Smith almost singlehandedly broke the back of the Washington Capitals during their 1985 playoff confrontation. In the final game of their three-out-of-five-game series, the super-competitive goalie stopped 39 shots. The Philadelphia Flyers prevented the Islanders from reaching their sixth straight Stanley Cup final in 1985, and may have ended an era for the gutsy Smith.

Intestinal fortitude is a character trait all good goalies must possess. Playing in goal in front of a large crowd can be a frightening experience. It's like going to the office and having 18,000 co-workers critically watching your every move. There's no hiding mistakes. Goals are accompanied by a flashing red light, sirens and the derisive

Figure 53. Former Hartford goaltender Greg Millen, now with the
St. Louis Blues, shows the butterfly style of goaltending popularized
by hall-of-famer Glen Hall, of the Chicago Black Hawks. Photo by J.
Henson Photographics.

comments of fans. Like many professional athletes, goaltenders are not as frightened of getting hurt as they are of embarrassing themselves.

Like Rodney Dangerfield, most goaltenders feel like they get no respect. If a team loses by one goal, even if the goalie has played exceptionally well, most of the fans will forget the saves and remember the goal that cost the game.

Most goalies are not superstars and many have the very real sensation of fighting for their jobs every time they take the ice. They are in constant fear that one bad goal or one period of poor play may lose them the job they've waited their whole lives to assume. Goalies are only as good as their last game and their last save. There is no room for resting on laurels from previous accomplishments.

Goaltenders, like other NHL regulars below all-star caliber, never want to leave a game because of a minor injury or the flu, not knowing when they'd be able to get back in. They know there's always someone waiting in the wings ready to pounce on the opportunity to take away their starting job. In what other sport do you see players go into the dressing room for stiches or because they have lost two or three teeth, and then return to the game?

The toothless, stitched-up visages of years past have been replaced by the matinee-idol good looks of some of today's stars. Nonetheless, hockey remains the most volatile of team sports. Fights break out with regularity, not the all-out, stick-swinging rumbles of years ago, but battles nonetheless.

It cannot be denied that for many fans, these skirmishes are the most enjoyable moments of the night. Tempers are sure to flare in contact sports. These mini-wars on the rink will occupy us next.

Chapter Thirteen

Fights on the Ice

In all contact sports that allow (within certain restrictions) one player to slam his body into another's, tempers surely will explode and frustrations will be vented. In no team sport, including football, do these battles occur with more regularity than in ice hockey.

Because of the speed provided by their skates, players crash at velocities reached in car wrecks. In addition, these ice warriors use their elbows, hips, knees and occasionally their sticks as weapons with which to duel and dole out punishment.

Today's NHL games average about one major confrontation per contest. Some teams seem to generate more than their share of battles and to evoke more dislike from peers than others. Rivalries between two clubs can lead to open hostility. In the past, certain squads became well known for their roughhousing tactics, drafted burly enforcers and viewed the numerous rumbles in their games as badges of courage.

Until recently, many American fans, who did not understand the intricacies of the sport as well as their Canadian counterparts, looked at fights as the most exciting ingredient to the game. But as U.S. spectators have grown in sophistication, they have learned to cheer displays of hockey skills and no longer come soley to watch players brawl.

Current NHL players are more highly educated, younger on the average, and better conditioned than those of a decade ago. Because of advancements in equipment already described, the game moves faster and is more offense oriented than in the past. Coaches cannot afford to keep an enforcer on the team at the expense of a player with more finesse.

Also, fines for misconduct are much more severe than in previous times. Players who receive three misconduct penalties are automatically suspended for the next league game, a serious setback if a team leader is involved. All of these factors have helped reduce the number of fights per game. Nonetheless, no rules can stop hot-headed players from exploding, or deny larger players the right to use their size to their advantage.

By their reputations, these guys make sure that no one will take a cheap shot without suffering the consequences. They disturb the concentration of rival team members, constantly wary that the enforcer has them in his sights and is ready to lower the boom with a vicious check.

One of the most famous of this group was John Ferguson, a winger on the Montreal Canadien teams of the late 1960s and early 1970s. Ferguson is now general manager of the Winnipeg Jets. Six-time MVP right wing Gordie Howe of the Detroit Red Wings, during the late 1940s until his retirement from the NHL in 1971, was another whose aggressive (some rivals claimed dirty) style became one of his trademarks (figure 54).

Howe's confrontational attitude and longevity is made all the more remarkable when one realizes that he nearly died from an injury caused by a headlong plunge into a wooden board, during a 1950 playoff game against the Toronto Maple Leafs. Not only did he come back from this disaster, but he led the league in scoring the following year.

Howe's stickhandling skills were matched by his ability to use his body and stick to punish opponents, without being detected by the officials. His head-to-head duels with Maurice Richard during the 1950s were among the most intense ever witnessed in the sport.

Dave Semenko, the 6-foot-3, 215-pound left wing for

Figure 54. **This archival 1956 photograph shows the legendary Gordie Howe at work. Notice his curveless stick.** Courtesy Detroit Red Wings.

the Edmonton Oilers, carries on in the tradition of a Dave Schultz, who played the same role on the Philadelphia Flyer Stanley-Cup-winning teams of 1973-74 and 1974-75. Semenko's presence on the ice makes rivals think twice before going after Gretzky.

Because it is difficult to punch with padded hockey gloves, players usually drop them as well as their sticks before striking an opponent. Most jabs are aimed at the face. But since almost all players now wear helmets, a broken hand can result from a misguided blow to the chops.

A common ruse is to take an opponent's sweater and pull it over his head before launching an attack. To combat this practice, trainers use a thick, elastic band on the inside of the sweater to tie down the jersey to the hockey pants.

During fights, fans will notice that players not directly involved in the altercation pair off with their nearest competitor. The intention here is to prevent two players from ganging up on one individual (figure 55).

Figure 55. **This scuffle in front of the New Jersey net followed a save by their goaltender.**

Figure 56. After a fight, linesmen try to cool tempers while the referee skates to the penalty box to dole out punishment.

Figure 57. Linesmen rush in to break up the fisticuffs as referee Kerry Fraser looks on.

Even if one of the combatants is clearly outmatched, his teammates must take care not to act as the third entrant into the fight. For doing so, they risk a game misconduct penalty. Linesmen, not the referee, stop the fight when one player clearly gains an advantage.

When a fight takes place, all uninvolved players are supposed to clear the zone in which the altercation occurs and move to areas designated by the referee. Referees may impose a major or a major and a game misconduct penalty on any player who starts a fight. A two-minute minor penalty can be charged against a skater, who having been struck, retaliates (figures 56 and 57).

Most fights result in both parties being assessed five-minute majors. Both teams may subsitute for the guilty players, who serve their time in the penalty box. Therefore, teams are generally not short handed after these altercations. Still, the players found guilty must remain in the penalty box for five minutes, even if a goal is scored against their team.

Hockey players, coaches and management accept these battles as inherent in the nature of the sport. It cannot be denied that there is a bit of the gladiator in most skaters. It can also not be denied that many fans get a charge when one of their home-team players gets in a good lick.

As long as the officials maintain a measure of control and can prevent serious injury, scuffles on the ice will be permitted. Completely outlawing fighting would only result in players holding on to and using their sticks, a far more dangerous alternative.

Chapter Fourteen

Hockey Injuries

In all contact sports that require players to hurl their bodies at one another, disregarding personal safety, injuries are an inevitable consequence. In ice hockey, participants reach great speeds on sharp-edged skates, wage battles on a rock-hard surface and grasp sticks that can cause serious damage. Bodies are frequently strained beyond their limits and painful wounds result.

Groin and hamstring pulls, the goaltender's nemesis, can put players out of action for months. Goalies, whose hands can swell from stopping pucks, also suffer from deep bruises to unprotected areas and from severe back maladies, the result of bone-crunching checks or butterfly-save maneuvers. Cuts to their faces have been markedly reduced since the introduction of caged masks.

On the other hand, the most common injury to forwards and defensemen, who skate without facial protection, is the cut or laceration, caused by sticks and deflected pucks. Team physicians and dentists, furnished to both sides by the host club, suture the less-serious wounds and players usually return to finish out the game. On the average, each player suffers one cut severe enough to warrant stiches, per year. Required use of the helmet and face mask have markedly limited these lacerations to hockey participants from the amateur ranks.

Possibly the most excruciating, common injuries are those associated with the knee. Torn ligaments and cartilage as well as dislocated kneecaps can keep players on disabled lists for sustained periods. Fractures and internal hemorrhaging are rare but not unknown to those engaged in the sport. Every year, one or two players from each team in the NHL will suffer a broken bone.

Painful blisters, which can develop from poor-fitting skates, bunions and calluses can debilitate or at least impair skaters. In the middle of the season, at the points on the feet where the laces go around the instep, sensitive areas can develop. Rashes and infections have also been known to cause aggravating problems.

One underreported but alarming development recently has been the increase in the number of spinal injuries incurred by hockey players. According to Dr. Charles Tator and Virginia Edmonds, writing in the April 1, 1984, Canadian Medical Association Journal, "Between September 1980 and October 1981, five hockey players with major spinal injuries, four of which were injuries to the cervical spinal cord, were treated at the acute spinal cord injury unit at Sunnybrook Medical Centre, Toronto. In contrast, between 1974, when the unit opened, and 1980 only one hockey player with a spinal injury was treated at the unit. Similarly, none of the 358 spinal cord injuries studied at two Toronto hospitals between 1948 and 1973 were hockey-related, and previous reports of hockey injuries included no cases of spinal cord injury."

Between 1976 and 1983, reported the authors, 42 players, with a median age of 17, received injuries falling into this category. Twenty eight of those were spinal-cord injuries and 17 resulted in complete paralysis below the vertebral level of the injury. "Strikes from behind and collisions with the boards were common mechanisms of injury. Many of the players had suffered a burst fracture of the cervical spine following a blow to the top of the helmet when the neck was slightly flexed," wrote the researchers.

A striking finding was that the vast majority of the 42 injuries did not occur in practice but rather in organized leagues, ranging from the Ontario Hockey Association to adult leagues. Thirty seven of the players were wearing helmets.

"A blow to the head from a push or check into the boards was the most common injury event," continued Tator and Edmonds. "Indeed, 13 of the 17 players who had been pushed or checked had been struck from behind, which strongly suggests that an alteration in the rules or enforcement of existing rules against attack from behind would be an important preventive measure. The unexpected impact does not allow the player to tense his muscles to resist the force of the impact.

"Most of the players had never done specific exercises to strengthen their neck muscles, and most claimed that they had never been advised by their coaches to do so. Most were also unaware of the added risk of impact in flexion, and none had been cautioned about the dangers of spearing."

Although this book was designed primarily for the hockey fan and not for the participant, many players, coaches and referees from the junior and amateur ranks will read this section. It seems wise, then, to publicize the conclusions of such an important safety study. The recommendations of Tator and Edmond follow:

1. "The hockey leagues should enforce the current rules, especially those against boarding and cross-checking, and should consider introducing new rules against pushing or checking from behind. They should also recommend muscle-conditioning programs to improve the strength of the neck muscles. They should avoid using small rinks and should maintain accurate statistics on the occurrence of severe injuries.

2. "The players should be educated about the possibility of major neck injuries. They should avoid spearing and impact, especially with the boards, when the neck is flexed. They should follow a neck-muscle-conditioning program and avoid using poorly fitting helmets.

3. "The equipment manufacturers should encourage and undertake research on helmet design, especially with regard to shape and shock absorbancy."

Jolts, collisions, bumps and bruises are a way of life on an ice hockey rink. Improved conditioning methods, better communication between those actively involved in the sport and following the appropriate recommendations of experts like those cited will enhance safety and make the game more fun for spectators and players alike.

Chapter Fifteen

Training Camp

Years ago, each NHL club had two or three minor-league farm teams and 60 to 70 players under contract. Although the minor leagues still thrive, clubs can no longer afford the luxury of supporting as many individuals as in the past. Two NHL franchises may now share one farm team.

Inspired by the high salary negotiated for Bobby Orr by his agent, Alan Eagleson, in 1966, hockey pros use experts to barter with management and salaries have escalated tremendously. As a result, general managers often sign only their first three draft choices and test unheralded rookies at training camps. Many released lower draft choices fail to latch on to a minor-league club.

NHL training camps differ substantially in character from those run by the NFL, where an important goal is to whip rookies and rusty veterans into shape. The NHL Players Association lobbied for and won from the owners a promise that training camps last no longer than three weeks. This concession made relics of special one-week rookie camps. The 45 or 50 players who show up must report in shape or face immediate release.

The 10 or 11 exhibition games start four days into the 21-day session, generally in mid-September. Within a few days, management pares down the roster to about 30 players, 20 for the big club and 10 relegated to the minors or to reserve positions. As in most professional sports, training camps usually are not held in the home town of the parent team. The prime factor here is not so much reduced rates for renting ice for practice. Rather, general managers hope to limit distractions for team members and to develop comraderie and cohesiveness within the squad.

On the camp's first day, players receive physicals and select equipment. About fifteen to 20% of the NHL regulars endorse sticks, skates and other related merchandise. Some may receive a few thousand dollars while others get hundreds of times that amount to promote a manufacturer's product.

Early on, players go through rigorous stretching routines. Coaches hope to help their charges prevent pulling muscles maintained, but seldom pushed to their limits, during the off-season. Recently, aerobics and fitness instructors have been brought in to improve player flexibility.

Skating drills are implemented and team members take turns handling and shooting pucks at the goaltenders. Practices run in two shifts, with one group staying on the ice from 8 to 10 am. The next group comes from 10:30 am to 12:30 pm. Afternoon practice, which generally includes a refereed scrimmage, resumes from 2 to 4 pm and from 4 to 6 pm, giving roster members about four hours on the ice per day. Usually, meetings are held in the evening to review the day's work.

Videotape and film do not occupy crucial roles in the NHL, unlike professional and collegiate football. All games are filmed, but rather than players having to sit through an examination of an entire game, coaches use clips to point out an individual's errors, weaknesses and strengths.

In the evening, the coaches and general manager get together and mull over the performances of the afternoon scrimmage. Primarily, management tries to determine which combinations of skaters (lines) work best on the ice. Like good chemists, they must create the team's character with players that will complement one another.

Team members who like to drink alcoholic beverages leave the hotel for dinner, since management does not approve of that practice. Evening curfews usually are set at 11 pm. Players car pool to practice for the morning workouts.

Fewer rituals are associated with NHL training camps than with their NFL counterparts. Rookies do not stand up and sing their college fight songs. Nonetheless, there remains the tradition of selecting one rookie a day and either shaving his head, cutting off half of his mustache or removing one sideburn.

Just as NFL teams may carry reserve or injured players on taxi squads, NHL teams may keep more than the 18 players and two goaltenders permitted to take part in regular-season games, which start around October 15th. These reserves serve to remind veterans that others anxiously wait in the wings to take their place on the roster.

Some superstars have multiyear, guaranteed contracts and have no such distractions. Many other regulars, of lesser ability, live on a tightrope. They never feel certain whether they are destined to toil for a minor-league franchise or are headed for a long ride in the glamorous, fast-speed lane laid out for the members of the NHL parent club.

Chapter Sixteen

Game Day

A few days after training camp concludes, the regular season opens. On game days both teams arrive at the arena at designated times in the morning and skate for 30 to 45 minutes, work up a sweat and loosen up. After practice, forwards and defensemen often go to the arena's carpentry workshop to have their sticks shortened or their stick-blade curves altered. In addition, before each game, trainers sharpen the players' skate blades. Goaltenders have that job performed less frequently.

Following the morning practice, players return to their homes or hotels. They may then have lunch, attend to business obligations, take naps or run errands. About 90 minutes before game time, the teams come back to their dressings rooms and prepare for pregame warm-ups. At this time, members of team fan clubs enter the rink and put up their signs and banners.

Pregame Warm-Ups

Players come out on the ice, loosen up and stretch for about 35 minutes before the scheduled game time. After a few minutes, the starting goalie enters the net. From about 40 feet away, each of his teammates then lines up with a puck and fires it at the goal (figure 58). The first goaltender on the ice is the one who will start the game (figure 59). After the shooting drills, the team goes through various skating and passing routines.

Figure 58.   Players fire shots at the goalie in the pregame warm-ups.

Figure 59.   The starting goaltender leads his team back to the ice.

Some players sign autographs during these warm-ups, but fans stand a better chance of getting a player's signature at the conclusion of the game. Before the opening face-off, ticket holders can stand behind one of the goal nets and see how fast the pucks travel. From this perspective, one quickly learns to appreciate the difficulty of the goaltender's task. At this time before the opening face-off, fans can also check on the progress of injured players, who may skate with the team during pregame warm-ups.

One note of caution seems prudent. Spectators should beware of pucks sailing over the plexiglass behind the nets. Unwary fans have occasionally been struck by these projectiles.

The Zamboni

Figure 60. Zamboni drivers scrape and resurface the ice before the game and between periods.

After players leave the ice, fans will notice a strange-looking, mobile contraption circling the rink. That machine, called a Zamboni, was first used by the Chicago Black Hawks and was a common fixture in NHL rinks by the early 1950s.

The Zamboni driver determines how much of the ice to shave off, depending on the weather and on the condition of the ice. A long razor attached to the back of the Zamboni skims along the ice surface. Then hot water, which binds well and makes a tight seal, is laid over the area. The towel which trails the machine, smooths out the surface (figure 60).

Next, a rink employee digs out two holes for the goal to be set into place (figure 61). Antifreeze is poured into the openings to prevent the magnetized screws from freezing. Magnetized goal posts are then put in place over the screws. The magnetic field created keeps the goal in place.

To prevent players from being impaled on an immovable goalpost, these breakaway goals which supposedly can withstand 200 pounds of pressure before releasing from their moorings, have been used with some success. One problem has arisen, though. Without much effort, certainly not 200 pounds of pressure, goaltenders have been able to push the posts off their settings. Further refinements will hopefully correct this problem.

One consequence of breakaway goalposts is that players feel safer crashing into these areas at far greater speeds than in the past. As a result, some analysts believe goaltenders have been slammed into more frequently and with more force than in the past. The improved safety of the skaters has, so far, outweighed this drawback.

Figure 61. One of the maintenance workers prepares the ice for the goal to be set on its magnetized moorings.

Last-Minute Preparations

While the ice crew performs its job, players remain in the dressing room, untie their skates and take a drink of soda or juice. The locker room's atmosphere is much quieter and more relaxed than those associated with football teams. No one audibly psyches up. Players know their jobs and mentally go over the coach's suggestions to them during the morning practice.

Before the game starts and at the referee's request, the visiting team's manager or coach supplies the referee or the official scorer with the starting lineup. That information is relayed to the home coach who then decides on a line to counter his opposition. His trainer then submits those names to the referee or official scorer, who takes the lineup to the visiting coach.

No changes in either lineup are allowed until the game starts. Breaking this rule may result in a minor penalty against the offending team.

Three minutes before game time, buzzers sound in both locker rooms and then ring once again when it is time to go out on the ice. Traditionally, the starting goaltender arrives first on the ice and then, according to a team's idiosyncractic superstitions, others follow in a prescribed order. No order of entry is mandated except on the season's opening day, when players are introduced by number.

Next comes the singing of the national anthem. When a Canadian team plays one from an American city, both national anthems are performed.

Only the chosen few advance all the way to the NHL, fulfilling lifelong dreams. All of us, for the price of a ticket, can sit in the stands and dream of exploits on the ice. Hopefully, this book has provided a taste of life in the fast lane of ice hockey and will become a valuable tool to those who never before understood how to watch this electrifying game.

Appendix A

Award and Trophy Winners

Stanley Cup Winners

Season	Champions		
1892-93	Montreal A.A.A.	1926-27	Ottawa Senators
1894-95	Montreal Victorias	1927-28	New York Rangers
1895-96	Winnipeg Victorias	1928-29	Boston Bruins
1896-97	Montreal Victorias	1929-30	Montreal Canadiens
1897-98	Montreal Victorias	1930-31	Montreal Canadiens
1898-99	Montreal Shamrocks	1931-32	Toronto Maple Leafs
1899-00	Montreal Shamrocks	1932-33	New York Rangers
1900-01	Winnipeg Victorias	1933-34	Chicago Black Hawks
1901-02	Montreal A.A.A.	1934-35	Montreal Maroons
1902-03	Ottawa Silver Seven	1935-36	Detroit Red Wings
1903-04	Ottawa Silver Seven	1936-37	Detroit Red Wings
1904-05	Ottawa Silver Seven	1937-38	Chicago Black Hawks
1905-06	Montreal Wanderers	1938-39	Boston Bruins
1906-07	Kenora Thistles (January)	1939-40	New York Rangers
1907-07	Montreal Wanderers (March)	1940-41	Boston Bruins
1907-08	Montreal Wanderers	1941-42	Toronto Maple Leafs
1908-09	Ottawa Senators	1942-43	Detroit Red Wings
1909-10	Montreal Wanderers	1943-44	Montreal Canadiens
1910-11	Ottawa Senators	1944-45	Toronto Maple Leafs
1911-12	Quebec Bulldogs	1945-46	Montreal Canadiens
1912-13	Quebec Bulldogs	1946-47	Toronto Maple Leafs
1913-14	Toronto Blue Shirts	1947-48	Toronto Maple Leafs
1914-15	Vancouver Millionaires	1948-49	Toronto Maple Leafs
1915-16	Montreal Canadiens	1949-50	Detroit Red Wings
1916-17	Seattle Metropolitans	1950-51	Toronto Maple Leafs
1917-18	Toronto Arenas	1951-52	Detroit Red Wings
1918-19	No Decision	1952-53	Montreal Canadiens
1919-20	Ottawa Senators	1953-54	Detroit Red Wings
1920-21	Ottawa Senators	1954-55	Detroit Red Wings
1921-22	Toronto St. Pats	1955-56	Montreal Canadiens
1922-23	Ottawa Senators	1956-57	Montreal Canadiens
1923-24	Montreal Canadiens	1957-58	Montreal Canadiens
1924-25	Victoria Cougars	1958-59	Montreal Canadiens
1925-26	Montreal Maroons	1959-60	Montreal Canadiens

1960-61	Chicago Black Hawks
1961-62	Toronto Maple Leafs
1962-63	Toronto Maple Leafs
1963-64	Toronto Maple Leafs
1964-65	Montreal Canadiens
1965-66	Montreal Canadiens
1966-67	Toronto Maple Leafs
1967-68	Montreal Canadiens
1968-69	Montreal Canadiens
1969-70	Boston Bruins
1970-71	Montreal Canadiens
1971-72	Boston Bruins
1972-73	Montreal Canadiens
1973-74	Philadelphia Flyers
1974-75	Philadelphia Flyers
1975-76	Montreal Canadiens
1976-77	Montreal Canadiens
1977-78	Montreal Canadiens
1978-79	Montreal Canadiens
1979-80	New York Islanders
1980-81	New York Islanders
1981-82	New York Islanders
1982-83	New York Islanders
1983-84	Edmonton Oilers
1984-85	Edmonton Oilers
1985-86	Montreal Canadiens

Art Ross Trophy

This trophy is presented to the player who scored the most points during the regular season. If players tie for the lead, the trophy goes to the one with the most goals. If still tied, it is given to the player with the fewer number of games played. If these measures do not break the deadlock, the trophy is won by the player who scored his first goal of the season, at the earliest date. Art Ross, the former manager coach of the Boston Bruins, presented the trophy to the NHL in 1947.

Season	Player and Club	Goals	Points
1917-18	Joe Malone, Mtl. Canadiens	44	44
1918-19	Newsy Lalonde, Mtl. Canadiens	23	32

Season	Player and Club	Goals	Points
1919-20	Joe Malone, Quebec	39	48
1920-21	Newsy Lalonde, Mtl. Canadiens	33	41
1921-22	Punch Broadbent, Ottawa	32	46
1922-23	Babe Dye, Toronto	26	37
1923-24	Cy Denneny, Ottawa	22	23
1924-25	Babe Dye, Toronto	38	44
1925-26	Nels Stewart, Montreal	34	42
1926-27	Bill Cook, N.Y. Rangers	33	37
1927-28	Howie Morenz, Mtl. Canadiens	33	51
1928-29	Ace Bailey, Toronto	22	32
1929-30	Cooney Weiland, Boston	43	73
1930-31	Howie Morenz, Mtl. Canadiens	28	51
1931-32	Harvey Jackson, Toronto	28	53
1932-33	Bill Cook, N.Y. Rangers	28	50
1933-34	Charlie Conacher, Toronto	32	52
1934-35	Charlie Conacher, Toronto	36	57
1935-36	Dave Schriner, N.Y. Americans	19	45
1936-37	Dave Schriner, N.Y. Americans	21	46
1937-38	Gordie Drillon, Toronto	26	52
1938-39	Toe Blake, Mtl. Canadiens	24	47
1939-40	Milt Schmidt, Boston	22	52
1940-41	Bill Cowley, Boston	17	62
1941-42	Bryan Hextall, N.Y. Rangers	24	56
1942-43	Doug Bentley, Chicago	33	73
1943-44	Cain, Boston	36	82
1944-45	Elmer Lach, Montreal	26	80
1945-46	Max Bentley, Chicago	31	61
1946-47	Max Bentley, Chicago	29	72
1947-48	Elmer Lach, Montreal	30	61
1948-49	Roy Conacher, Chicago	26	68
1949-50	Ted Lindsay, Detroit	23	78
1950-51	Gordie Howe, Detroit	43	86
1951-52	Gordie Howe, Detroit	47	86
1952-53	Gordie Howe, Detroit	49	95
1953-54	Gordie Howe, Detroit	33	81
1954-55	Bernie Geoffrion, Montreal	38	75
1955-56	Jean Beliveau, Montreal	47	88
1956-57	Gordie Howe, Detroit	44	89
1957-58	Dickie Moore, Montreal	36	84
1958-59	Dickie Moore, Montreal	41	96
1959-60	Bobby Hull, Chicago	39	81
1960-61	Bernie Geoffrion, Montreal	50	95
1961-62	Bobby Hull, Chicago	50	84
1962-63	Gordie Howe, Detroit	38	86
1963-64	Stan Mikita, Chicago	39	89
1964-65	Stan Mikita, Chicago	28	87

Season	Player and Club	Goals	Points
1965-66	Bobby Hull,Chicago	54	97
1966-67	Stan Mikita, Chicago	35	97
1967-68	Stan Mikita, Chicago	40	87
1968-69	Phil Esposito, Boston	49	126
1969-70	Bobby Orr, Boston	33	120
1970-71	Phil Esposito, Boston	76	152
1971-72	Phil Esposito, Boston	66	133
1972-73	Phil Esposito, Boston	55	130
1973-74	Phil Esposito, Boston	68	145
1974-75	Bobby Orr, Boston	46	135
1975-76	Guy Lafleur, Montreal	56	125
1976-77	Guy Lafleur, Montreal	56	136
1977-78	Guy Lafleur, Montreal	60	132
1978-79	Bryan Tottier, New York Islanders	47	134
1979-80	Marcel Dionne, Los Angeles	53	137
1980-81	Wayne Gretzky, Edmonton	55	164
1981-82	Wayne Gretzky, Edmonton	92	212
1982-83	Wayne Gretzky, Edmonton	71	196
1983-84	Wayne Gretzky, Edmonton	87	205
1984-85	Wayne Gretzky, Edmonton	73	208
1985-86	Wayne Gretzky, Edmonton	52	215

Calder Memorial Trophy

This trophy is awarded to the NHL's top rookie, who is selected by a vote of hockey writers and broadcasters in each of the 21 NHL cities. The trophy was originated in 1937 by Frank Calder, first president of the league. After his death in 1943, the league presented the Calder Memorial Trophy in his memory. Eligible players cannot have participated in more than 20 games in any preceding season or in six or more games in each of any two preceding seasons.

1932-33	Carl Voss, Detroit	
1933-34	Russ Blinco, Montreal M.	
1934-35	Dave Schriner, New York A.	
1935-36	Mike Karakas, Chicago	
1936-37	Syl Apps, Toronto	
1937-38	Cully Dahlstrom, Chicago	

1938-39	Frank Brimsek, Boston
1939-40	Kilby MacDonald, New York R.
1940-41	Johnny Quilty, Montreal C.
1941-42	Grant Warwick, New York R.
1942-43	Gaye Stewart, Toronto
1943-44	Gus Bodnar, Toronto
1944-45	Frank McCool, Toronto
1945-46	Edgar Laprade, New York R.
1946-47	Howie Meeker, Toronto
1947-48	Jim McFadden, Detroit
1948-49	Pentti Lund, New York R.
1949-50	Jack Gelineau, Boston
1950-51	Terry Sawchuk, Detroit
1951-52	Bernie Geoffrion, Montreal
1952-53	Lorne Worsley, New York R.
1953-54	Camille Henry, New York R.
1954-55	Ed Litzenberger, Chicago
1955-56	Glenn Hall, Detroit
1956-57	Larry Regan, Boston
1957-58	Frank Mahovlich, Toronto
1958-59	Ralph Backstrom, Montreal
1959-60	Bill Hay, Chicago
1960-61	Dave Keon, Toronto
1961-62	Bobby Rousseau, Montreal
1962-63	Kent Douglas, Toronto
1963-64	Jacques Laperriere, Montreal
1964-65	Roger Crozier, Detroit
1965-66	Brit Selby, Toronto
1966-67	Bobby Orr, Boston
1967-68	Derek Sanderson, Boston
1968-69	Danny Grant, Minnesota
1969-70	Tony Esposito, Chicago
1970-71	Gil Perreault, Buffalo
1971-72	Ken Dryden, Montreal
1972-73	Steve Vickers, New York R.
1973-74	Denis Potvin, New York I.
1974-75	Eric Vail, Atlanta
1975-76	Bryan Trottier, New York I.
1976-77	Willi Plett, Atlanta
1977-78	Mike Bossy, New York I.
1978-79	Bobby Smith, Minnesota
1979-80	Ray Bourque, Boston
1980-81	Peter Stastny, Quebec
1981-82	Dale Hawerchuk, Winnipeg
1982-83	Steve Larmer, Chicago
1983-84	Tom Barrasso, Buffalo
1984-85	Mario Lemieux, Pittsburgh
1985-86	Gary Suter, Calgary

Hart Memorial Trophy

This trophy is awarded to the NHL's most valuable player. Selected by hockey writers and broadcasters from each of the 21 NHL cities, the award was presented by the NHL in 1960 after the original Hart Trophy was retired to the Hockey Hall of Fame. The original Hart Trophy was donated in 1923 by Dr. David A. Hart, father of Cecil Hart, former manager-coach of the Montreal Canadiens.

1923-24	Frank Nighbor, Ottawa
1924-25	Billy Burch, Hamilton
1925-26	Nels Stewart, Montreal M.
1926-27	Herb Gardiner, Montreal C.
1927-28	Howie Morenz, Montreal C.
1928-29	Roy Worters, New York A.
1929-30	Nels Stewart, Montreal M.
1930-31	Howie Morenz, Montreal C.
1931-32	Howie Morenz, Montreal C.
1932-33	Eddie Shore, Boston
1933-34	Aurel Joliat, Montreal C.
1934-35	Eddie Shore, Boston
1935-36	Eddie Shore, Boston
1936-37	Babe Siebert, Montreal C.
1937-38	Eddie Shore, Boston
1938-39	Toe Blake, Montreal C.
1939-40	Eddie Goodfellow, Detroit
1940-41	Bill Cowley, Boston
1941-42	Tommy Anderson, New York A.
1942-43	Bill Cowley, Boston
1943-44	Babe Pratt, Toronto
1944-45	Elmer Lach, Montreal C.
1945-46	Max Bentley, Chicago
1946-47	Maurice Richard, Montreal
1947-48	Buddy O'Conner, New York R.
1948-49	Sid Abel, Detroit
1949-50	Charlie Rayner, New York R.
1950-51	Milt Schmidt, Boston
1951-52	Gordie Howe, Detroit
1952-53	Gordie Howe, Detroit

1953-54	Al Rollins, Chicago
1954-55	Ted Kennedy, Toronto
1955-56	Jean Beliveau, Montreal
1956-57	Gordie Howe, Detroit
1957-58	Gordie Howe, Detroit
1958-59	Andy Bathgate, New York R.
1959-60	Gordie Howe, Detroit
1960-61	Bernie Geoffrion, Montreal
1961-62	Jacques Plante, Montreal
1962-63	Gordie Howe, Detroit
1963-64	Jean Beliveau, Montreal
1964-65	Bobby Hull, Chicago
1965-66	Bobby Hull, Chicago
1966-67	Stan Mikita, Chicago
1967-68	Stan Mikita, Chicago
1968-69	Phil Esposito, Boston
1969-70	Bobby Orr, Boston
1970-71	Bobby Orr, Boston
1971-72	Bobby Orr, Boston
1972-73	Bobby Clarke, Philadelphia
1973-74	Phil Esposito, Boston
1974-75	Bobby Clarke, Philadelphia
1975-76	Bobby Clarke, Philadelphia
1976-77	Guy Lafleur, Montreal
1977-78	Guy Lafleur, Montreal
1978-79	Bryan Trottier, New York I.
1979-80	Wayne Gretzky, Edmonton
1980-81	Wayne Gretzky, Edmonton
1981-82	Wayne Gretzky, Edmonton
1982-83	Wayne Gretzky, Edmonton
1983-84	Wayne Gretzky, Edmonton
1984-85	Wayne Gretzky, Edmonton
1985-86	Wayne Gretzky, Edmonton

William M. Jennings Award

This award goes to the goalies for the team which gave the fewest goals during the regular season. Eligible goalies must have played at least 25 games. The trophy was presented to the NHL in 1982 in memory of William M. Jennings, an architect of the league's expansion from six teams to 21.

1981-82	Denis Herron, Montreal
	Rick Wamsley, Montreal
1982-83	Billy Smith, New York I.
	Roland Melanson, New York I.
1983-84	Al Jensen, Washington
	Pat Riggin, Washington
1984-85	Tom Barrasso, Buffalo
	Bob Sauve, Buffalo
1985-86	Bob Froese, Philadelphia
	David Jensen, Philadelphia

Lady Byng Trophy

This award, selected by a vote of hockey writers and broadcasters in the 21 NHL cities, goes to the player judged best at combining sportsmanship and playing ability. Lady Byng, the wife of the Governor-General of Canada in 1925, presented the trophy to the NHL during that year.

1924-25	Frank Nighbor, Ottawa
1925-26	Frank Nighbor, Ottawa
1926-27	Billy Burch, New York A.
1927-28	Frank Boucher, New York R.
1928-29	Frank Boucher, New York R.
1929-30	Frank Boucher, New York R.
1930-31	Frank Boucher, New York R.
1931-32	Joe Primeau, Toronto
1932-33	Frank Boucher, New York R.

1933-34	Frank Boucher, New York R.
1934-35	Frank Boucher, New York R.
1935-36	Doc Romnes, Chicago
1936-37	Marty Barry, Detroit
1937-38	Gordie Drillon, Toronto
1938-39	Clint Smith, New York R.
1939-40	Bobby Bauer, Boston
1940-41	Bobby Bauer, Boston
1941-42	Syl Apps, Toronto
1942-43	Max Bentley, Chicago
1943-44	Clint Smith, Chicago
1944-45	Bill Mosienko, Chicago
1945-46	Toe Blake, Montreal
1946-47	Bobby Bauer, Boston
1947-48	Buddy O'Connor, New York R.
1948-49	Bill Quackenbush, Detroit
1949-50	Edgar Laprade, New York R.
1950-51	Red Kelly, Detroit
1951-52	Sid Smith, Toronto
1952-53	Red Kelly, Detroit
1953-54	Red Kelly, Detroit
1954-55	Sid Smith, Toronto
1955-56	Earl Reibel, Detroit
1956-57	Andy Hebenton, New York R.
1957-58	Camille Henry, New York R.
1958-59	Alex Delvecchio, Detroit
1959-60	Don McKenney, Boston
1960-61	Red Kelly, Detroit
1961-62	Dave Keon, Toronto
1962-63	Dave Keon, Toronto
1963-64	Ken Wharram, Chicago
1964-65	Bobby Hull, Chicago
1965-66	Alex Delvecchio, Detroit
1966-67	Stan Mikita, Chicago
1967-68	Stan Mikita, Chicago
1968-69	Alex Delvecchio, Detroit
1969-70	Phil Goyette, St. Louis
1970-71	Johnny Bucyk, Boston
1971-72	Jean Ratelle, New York R.
1972-73	Gil Perreault, Buffalo
1973-74	John Bucyk, Boston
1974-75	Marcel Dionne, Detroit
1975-76	Jean Ratelle, New York R.
1976-77	Marcel Dionne, Los Angeles
1977-78	Butch Goring, Los Angeles
1978-79	Bob MacMillan, Atlanta

1979-80	Wayne Gretzky, Edmonton
1980-81	Rick Kehoe, Pittsburgh
1981-82	Rick Middleton, Boston
1982-83	Mike Bossy, New York I.
1983-84	Mike Bossy, New York I.
1984-85	Jari Kurri, Edmonton
1985-86	Mike Bossey, New York I.

Conn Smythe Trophy

This trophy is given to the MVP in the Stanley Cup playoffs selected in a vote of the league governors. The trophy was presented by Maple Leaf Gardens Ltd. in 1964 to honor the former coach, manager, president and owner of the Toronto Maple Leafs.

1964-65	Jean Beliveau, Montreal
1965-66	Roger Crozier, Detroit
1966-67	Dave Keon, Toronto
1967-68	Glenn Hall, St. Louis
1968-69	Serge Savard, Montreal
1969-70	Bobby Orr, Boston
1970-71	Ken Dryden, Montreal
1971-72	Bobby Orr, Boston
1972-73	Yvan Cournoyer, Montreal
1973-74	Bernie Parent, Philadelphia
1974-75	Bernie Parent, Philadelphia
1975-76	Reggie Leach, Philadelphia
1976-77	Guy Lafleur, Montreal
1977-78	Larry Robinson, Montreal
1978-79	Bob Gainey, Montreal
1979-80	Bryan Trottier, New York I.
1980-81	Butch Goring, New York I.
1981-82	Mike Bossy, New York I.
1982-83	Billy Smith, New York I.
1983-84	Mark Messier, Edmonton
1984-85	Wayne Gretzky, Edmonton
1985-86	Patrick Roy, Montreal

James Norris Memorial Trophy

This trophy is awarded to the league's best defense-man, who is selected by a vote of hockey writers and broadcasters in each of the 21 NHL cities. The trophy was presented in 1953 by the children of James Norris Sr., in memory of the former owner-president of the Detroit Red Wings.

1953-54	Red Kelly, Detroit
1954-55	Doug Harvey, Montreal
1955-56	Doug Harvey, Montreal
1956-57	Doug Harvey, Montreal
1957-58	Doug Harvey, Montreal
1958-59	Tom Johnson, Montreal
1959-60	Doug Harvey, Montreal
1960-61	Doug Harvey, Montreal
1961-62	Doug Harvey, New York R.
1962-63	Pierre Pilote, Chicago
1963-64	Pierre Pilote, Chicago
1964-65	Pierre Pilote, Chicago
1965-66	Jacques Laperriere, Montreal
1966-67	Harry Howell, New York R
1967-68	Bobby Orr, Boston
1968-69	Bobby Orr, Boston
1969-70	Bobby Orr, Boston
1970-71	Bobby Orr, Boston
1971-72	Bobby Orr, Boston
1972-73	Bobby Orr, Boston
1973-74	Bobby Orr, Boston
1974-75	Bobby Orr, Boston
1975-76	Denis Potvin, New York I.
1976-77	Larry Robinson, Montreal
1977-78	Denis Potvin, New York I.
1978-79	Denis Potvin, New York I.
1979-80	Larry Robinson, Montreal
1980-81	Randy Carlyle, Pittsburgh
1981-82	Doug Wilson, Chicago
1982-83	Rod Langway, Washington
1983-84	Rod Langway, Washington
1984-85	Paul Coffey, Edmonton
1985-86	Paul Coffey, Edmonton

All-Time NHL Records
(prior to the 1984-85 season)

Most Goals in One Game: 7, Joe Malone, Quebec Bulldogs, Jan. 31, 1920 vs. Toronto St. Pats; (Modern) 6, Syd Howe, Detroit Red Wings, Feb. 3, 1944 vs. New York Rangers; 6, Red Berenson, St. Louis Blues, Nov. 7, 1976 vs. Philadelphia Flyers; 6, Darryl Sittler, Toronto Maple Leafs, Feb. 7, 1976 vs. Boston Bruins.

Most Assists in One Game: 7, Bill Taylor, Detroit Red Wings, Mar 16, 1947 vs. Chicago Black Hawks; Wayne Gretzky, Edmonton, Feb. 15, 1980 vs. Washington Capitals.

Most Points in One Game: 10, Darryl Sittler, Toronto Maple Leafs, Feb. 7, 1976 vs. Boston Bruins (six goals, four assists)

Most Penalty Minutes in One Game: 67, Randy Holt, Los Angeles Kings, Mar. 11, 1979 vs. Philadelphia Flyers.

Most Goals in One Season: 92, Wayne Gretzky, Edmonton Oilers, 1981-82.

Most Assists in One Season: 125, Wayne Gretzky, Edmonton Oilers, 1982-83.

Most Points in One Season: 212, Wayne Gretzky, Edmonton Oilers, 1982-83.

Most Shutouts in One Season: 22, George Hainsworth, Montreal Canadiens, 1928-29; (Modern) 15, Tony Esposito, Chicago Black Hawks, 1969-70.

Most Penalty Minutes in One Season: 472, Dave Schultz, Philadelphia Flyers, 1974-75.

Most Points by a Rookie in One Season: 109, Peter Stastny, Quebec Nordiques, 1980-81.

Most Assists by a Goalie in One Season: 8, Mike Palmateer, Washington Capitals, 1980-81.

Most Seasons in a Career: 26, Gordie Howe, Detroit Red Wings, Hartford Whalers, 1946-47 to 1970-71, 1979-80.

Most Career Games: 1,767, Gordie Howe, Detroit Red Wings, Hartford Whalers.

Most Goals in a Career: 801, Gordie Howe, Detroit Red Wings, Hartford Whalers.

Most Career Points: 1,850, Gordie Howe, Detroit Red Wings, Hartford Whalers.

Most Penalty Minutes in a Career: 2,994, Dave Williams, Toronto, Vancouver, 1974-84.

Most Career Shutouts: 103, Terry Sawchuk, Detroit, Boston, Toronto, Los Angeles, New York Rangers.

Most Consecutive Gam   in a Career: 914, Garry Unger, Toronto, Detroit, St. Louis, Atlanta, Feb. 24, 1968 through Dec. 21, 1979.

National Collegiate Athletic Association Champions

Rensselaer Polytechnic Institute (RPI), which last took the title in 1954, won the 1985 NCAA playoffs and finished its year with a 35-2-1 record and a 33-game unbeaten streak. The Engineers' Neil Hernberg scored on a power play and teammate George Servinis (signed by the Minnesota North Stars) added a short-handed goal to pace RPI to a 2-1 victory over Providence. The Friars, in their first NCAA championship game, ended their season with a 23-17-5 record.

Year	Champion		
1948	Michigan	1967	Cornell
1949	Boston College	1968	Denver
1950	Colorado College	1969	Denver
1951	Michigan	1970	Cornell
1952	Michigan	1971	Boston University
1953	Michigan	1972	Boston University
1954	Rensselaer Poly	1973	Wisconsin
1955	Michigan	1974	Minnesota
1956	Michigan	1975	Michigan Tech
1957	Colorado College	1976	Minnesota
1958	Denver	1977	Wisconsin
1959	North Dakota	1978	Boston University
1960	Denver	1979	Minnesota
1961	Denver	1980	North Dakota
1962	Michigan Tech	1981	Wisconsin
1963	North Dakota	1982	North Dakota
1964	Michigan	1983	Wisconsin
1965	Michigan Tech	1984	Bowling Green
1966	Michigan State	1985	Rensselaer Poly
		1986	Michigan State

NHL Booster and Fan Clubs

Boston Bruins Fan Club
c/o Janet LePage
144 Rounds Street
New Bedford, MA 02140

Buffalo Sabres Booster Club
c/o Memorial Auditorium
140 Main Street
Buffalo, NY 14204

Calgary Flames
c/o Rick Skaggs
The Saddledome
Box 1540/Station M
Calgary, Alberta
T2P 3B9, Canada

Chicago Black Hawks
Standbys
c/o Chicago Stadium
1800 West Madison Street
Chicago,IL 60612

Detroit Red Wings for 'em
Club
Joe Louis Sports Arena
600 Civic Center Drive
Detroit, MI 48226

Edmonton Oilers Booster
Club
Box 11713
Edmonton, Alberta T5J 3K8
Canada

Hartford Whalers Booster
Club
P.O. Box 273
Hartford, CT 06141

Los Angeles Kings Booster
Club
c/o The Forum
P.O. Box 10
Inglewood, CA 90306

Minnesota North Stars
Met Center
7901 Cedar Avenue South
Bloomington, MN 55420

Montreal Canadiens
Gerard Frenchette
Fan Club Canadiens
2960 Goyer—#302
Montreal H3S 1H5
Canada

New Jersey Devil's Fan Club
c/o Edward Nudge
130 First Avenue
Port Reading, NJ 07064

New York Islanders Booster
Club
P.O. Box 20
Carle Place, NY 11514

New York Rangers Fan Club
G. P. O. Box 1772
New York, NY 10001

Philadelphia Flyers Fan
Club
The Spectrum
Broad Street and Pattison
Avenue
Philadelphia, PA 19148

Pittsburgh Penguins Fan Club
P.O. Box 903
Pittsburgh, PA 15230

Quebec Nordiques
c/o Michele Lapointe
Quebec Colisee
5555 Third Avenue, W
Charlesbourg, Quebec
G1H 6R1, Canada

St. Louis Blueliners
c/o Mary Ann Morcom
5418 Langsworth Drive
St. Louis, MO 63129

Toronto Maple Leafs
c/o Stan Obodiac
Maple Leaf Gardens
60 Carlton Street
Toronto, Ontario
M5B 1L1, Canada

Vancouver Canucks Booster Club
c/o John Arneil
#5—2324 West Broadway
Vancouver, British Columbia
V6R 2E5, Canada

Washington Capitals Fan Club
P.O. Box 306
Lanham, MD 20706

Winnipeg Jets Booster Club
c/o Winnipeg Arena
15-1430 Maroons Road
Winnipeg, Manitoba
R3G 0L5, Canada

Index

Page

158